Hanging Gardens

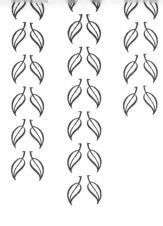

Hanging Gardens

By *JACK KRAMER*

Basket Plants, Indoors and Out

Drawings by CHARLES HOEPPNER
(unless otherwise noted)

CHARLES SCRIBNER'S SONS
New York

BOOKS BY JACK KRAMER IN THIS SERIES

Water Gardening
Miniature Plants Indoors and Out
Garden Planning for the Small Property
Hanging Gardens
(other titles in preparation)

Contents ✍

Diagrams and Drawings ✑

Hanging Gardens

Introduction: Gardens in the Air 🖋

Today, there are hundreds of lovely trailing and cascading plants to glorify your home and add glamour to outdoor rooms and patios. Some of them such as Philodendrons and Chlorophytums are old favorites; others such as cascading Petunias and Chrysanthemums are new. And there are Orchids, Ferns, Begonias, Geraniums, and Fuchsias to add to the colorful harvest of basket plants. Actually, almost any plant can be trained to basket-growing and experimenting is part of the fun of this kind of gardening.

Ten years ago, wire baskets were the only containers for these plants and the gardener had to make his own devices to suspend plants from ceilings. Now, we have many ornamental containers—ceramic, fiberglass, wooden—and sophisticated types of hardware to hang them. Most important, the annoyance of dripping water staining floors which so long kept basket plants outdoors, has been solved. There are many drip-trays and saucers to catch excess water.

The basket plant has come of age and with it a new world of gardening. A plant at eye level is in an enviable position to enjoy light from windows and fills otherwise barren space. It is also a display plant for it is immediately seen, never hidden at windows or in floor planters.

Like any other plant, trailers need trimming and potting, watering and feeding to grow well. It is also important to select plants for the conditions you can give them—shade, sun, bright light—and there are species for all exposures. Some plants are big and bold, others delicate and lacy and there are kinds for all interiors or for outdoor accent.

Some of the best trailing plants come from the Geranium, Fuchsia, and Begonia families and these are given special consideration in this book. Other lesser-known plants are not neglected and new ones are cited, some 200 varieties described here.

However, this is not only a book of descriptions and lists of plants; it is a complete compendium on the advantages of cascading plants and how to grow them successfully and use them intelligently for effective decoration, indoors and outside.

Jack Kramer

1. The Beauty of Basket Plants ✐

Trailing plants that brim over pot edges and sometimes cover a container with bright color enrich any indoor or outdoor area. Also effective in baskets, although not true trailers, are such plants as graceful Ferns, with their pendant fronds dripping over the container in a fountain of green, bushy Impatiens, covering the basket in a cloud of red flowers, and Chrysanthemums, Caladiums, and Coleus. In fact, almost any compact plant of bushy habit can be grown in a basket.

Plants in hanging containers grow better than plants on windowsills because of their many advantages; air circulates around the pot, light is good, and at eye level, the plants are easily seen from all sides.

WHERE TO PUT BASKET PLANTS

There is no set place for cascading plants. Indoors, put them where you need interest—some colorful flowers to brighten a corner or a lush display of green to complement a bare wall. Generally, hanging baskets should be placed at the perimeter of a room and suspended with chains, ropes, wire, raffia, or fish netting that are attached to eyehooks set into the ceiling. Baskets can be used also as pot plants on pedestal tables or stands without ceiling supports. Indeed, there are some handsome contemporary plant stands that adorned with cascading plants become a room feature. (See Chapter 4.)

Avoid placing pendant growers on windowsills or shelves; they are simply not attractive there and are more a bother than a beautiful

Graceful and airy, a fern furnishes needed vertical accent in author's living room. Container is a clay pot with drip-saucer attached. (Joyce R. Wilson photo)

accent. The circular form of the plant is thwarted by the pane of glass, and the plant appears lopsided. The rosette growth of many trailers is a unique attraction and should be viewed from all angles to be completely appreciated.

Outdoors, on the patio, porch, or terrace, there is no better decoration than trailers in ornamental containers. Suspend them from standards, porch ceilings, wooden or metal tripods, tree branches, or eaves; hang them from brackets or clip-on hangers from walls, fences, or posts. (See Drawing #1.)

A garden room is a natural place for hanging plants; orchids, tradescantia and chlorophytum decorate this scene. (Author photo)

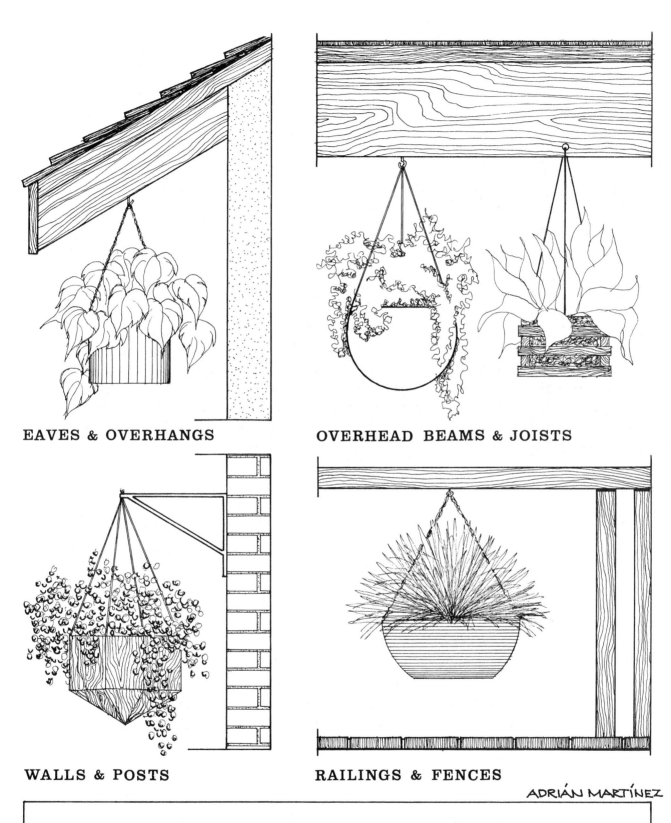

EAVES & OVERHANGS

OVERHEAD BEAMS & JOISTS

WALLS & POSTS

RAILINGS & FENCES

ADRIÁN MARTÍNEZ

Hanging Plants on the Exterior

Cascading ferns and orchids are part of this outdoor room that creates a lovely greenery. (Hort Pix Photo)

Although there are hundreds of foliage plants—old favorites, new ones, and overlooked species—for basket growing, there are also many fine flowering kinds. Dipladenias with charming pink blooms, Petunias in an array of colors, Orchid Cactus with mammoth flowers, Sedums, and Aeoniums—all are part of the cascading-plant picture. And they are no more difficult to grow than windowsill plants, because since they have light from all sides, they are usually easier to bring to perfection.

Top right: *Asparagus sprengeri is the vertical accent in this patio area.* (California Redwood Assoc. photo)

Bottom right: *A swimming pool becomes a tropical haven with trailing bromeliads on lattice work.* (Hedrich Blessing photo, Martin Bros. Builders)

BASKETS AND HANGING DEVICES

Any container can serve as a basket for plants: a bucket brimming with Petunias, a slatted wooden box flowing with lavender Orchids, or even a coconut shell with a lacy Philodendron. There is a limitless choice of pots and tubs governed only by your imagination, and there are dozens of commercial containers for plants. (See Chapter 2.)

Commercial containers are either opensided, with spaces between the wires or wooden battens, or standard clay or plastic pots. Plants such as Orchids and Christmas Cactus thrive in opensided containers because they should not be too moist at any time, and air circulating around the plant dries out soil quickly. The wire or wooden basket is best outdoors rather than indoors because it is difficult to attach saucers to them to catch dripping water.

Remember that hanging baskets filled with soil and plants are heavy and thus strong supports are needed. Hardware stores carry eyebolts, screweyes, brackets, and other ceiling hanging devices to hold the chain or rope that supports the container.

Some pots have holes drilled in the sides about an inch from the rim. Use wire or chain hangers, available at nurseries, for these pots. The wires are looped through the small holes, and the chain or wire is suspended from ceiling hooks. There are also clip-on hangers with wire or chain; these hangers grasp the edge of the pot firmly, and the wire or chain triangle is set into a hook. (See Drawing #2.)

Whatever kind of container you use indoors, attach an aluminum tray or clay saucer to it to catch excess water. These trays come in many depths and sizes and attach to the bottom of the pot. (See Chapter 2.)

PLANTING THE CONTAINERS

Slatted or wire containers can be lined with sphagnum moss; this material comes in sheets or shredded. Simply moisten the moss, and press it firmly against the sides of the container. You can also use osmunda cut into thin sheets and pressed into place. If soil sifting through the liner drops on the floors, set a layer of plastic or aluminum foil over the sphagnum or osmunda. Punch small holes in the material so that water can escape. (See Drawing #4.)

A standard greenhouse soil can be used for most plants; I use 1 part garden loam, 1 part sand, and 1 part leaf mold. For Succulents

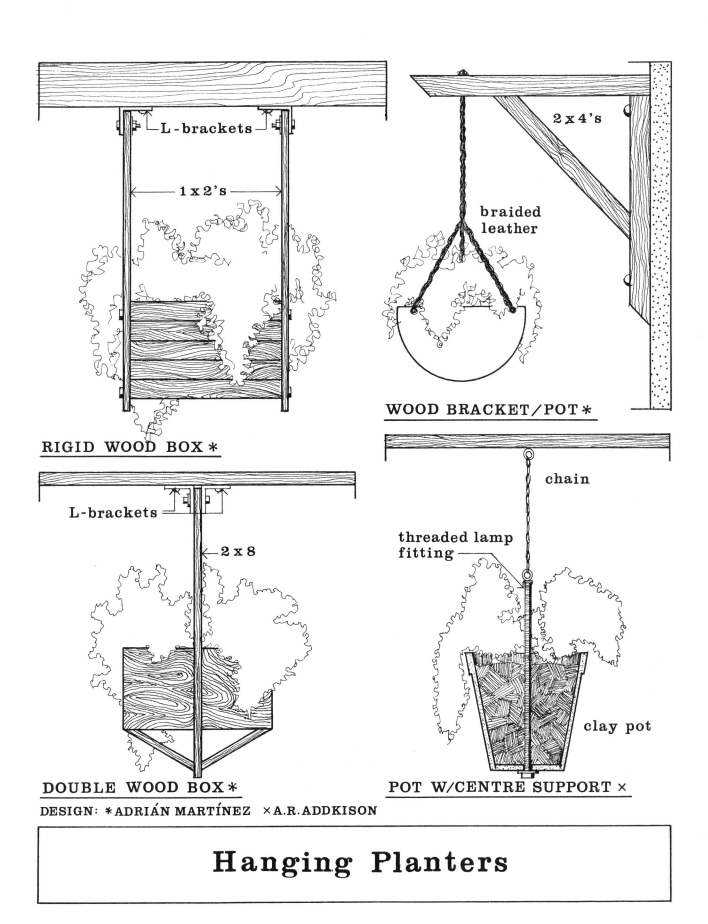

L-brackets

1 x 2's

RIGID WOOD BOX *

2 x 4's

braided leather

WOOD BRACKET/POT *

L-brackets

2 x 8

DOUBLE WOOD BOX *

chain

threaded lamp fitting

clay pot

POT W/CENTRE SUPPORT ×

DESIGN: *ADRIÁN MARTÍNEZ ×A.R.ADDKISON

Hanging Planters

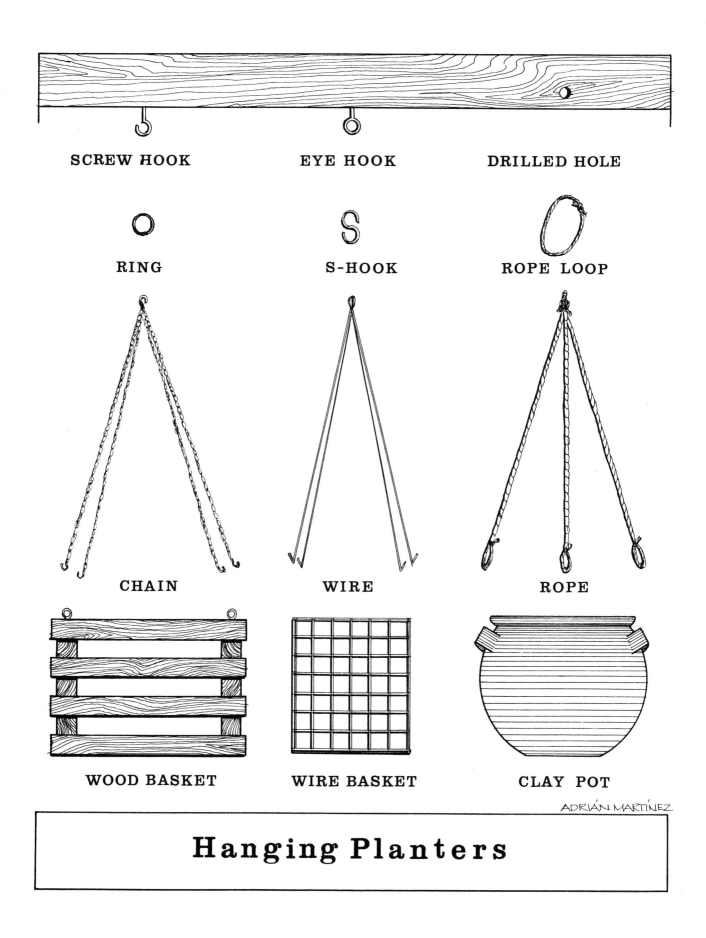

SCREW HOOK EYE HOOK DRILLED HOLE

RING S-HOOK ROPE LOOP

CHAIN WIRE ROPE

WOOD BASKET WIRE BASKET CLAY POT

ADRIÁN MARTÍNEZ

Hanging Planters

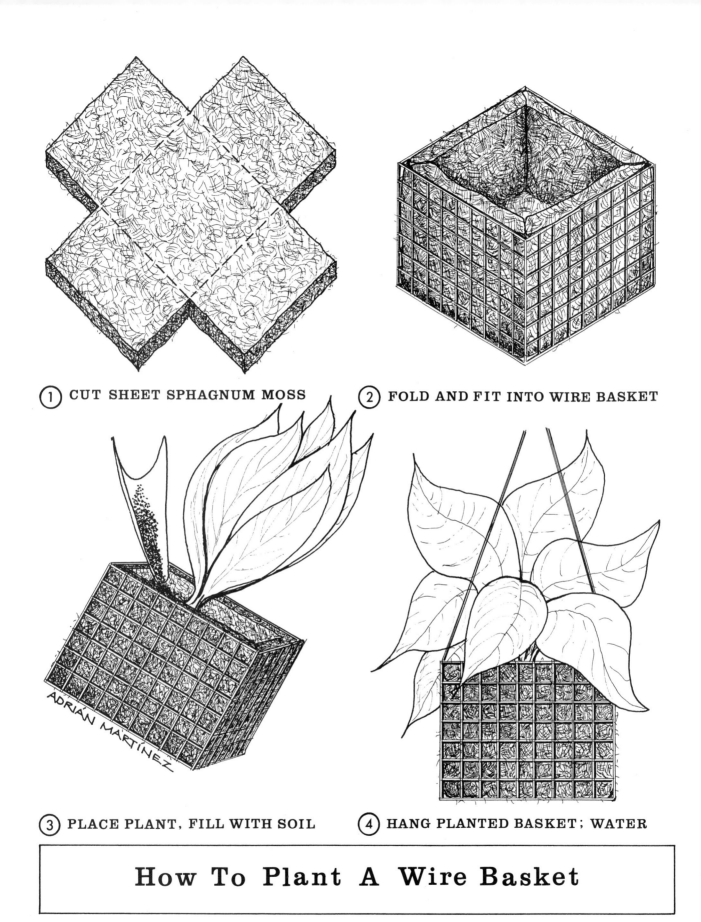

1 CUT SHEET SPHAGNUM MOSS

2 FOLD AND FIT INTO WIRE BASKET

ADRIAN MARTINEZ

3 PLACE PLANT, FILL WITH SOIL

4 HANG PLANTED BASKET; WATER

How To Plant A Wire Basket

and Cacti, I add more sand, and for Orchids and Bromeliads, I use fir bark. (This bark comes from the Douglas fir tree. It is steamed and chopped into sizes from ¼ to 1 inch in diameter and is available in sacks at most suppliers.) Put drainage materials (small pieces of broken pots) in the bottom of the container (not needed for open-sided baskets), and fill with a 2- to 3-inch bed of soil. Set plants on this foundation, and fill in and around with more soil, keeping the level about an inch below the top of the basket.

Some gardeners set small potted plants in baskets and cover the tops with sphagnum moss. This method cuts down planting time, and it is easy to refurbish the basket if necessary. However, it restricts plant growth. It is a better idea to remove plants from their clay pots and set them directly into the soil, as they then do not dry out as rapidly as plants left in pots, and it is easier to make a planting design with them.

2. *Containers for Plants* ✍

A few years ago, a container for trailing plants had to be a wire basket or a homemade one; little else was available. Now, an array of tubs, pots, and dishes, including standard clay pots that can be suspended from ceiling wires, are available at nurseries. There are also wall-mounted containers that can be placed at any desired height to accommodate trailing plants. And if you are handy with tools, new woods and plastics give you an opportunity to fashion your own containers for cascading plants.

To catch dripping water, dishes, pans, and saucers of clay or plastic are part of the new scene too. Most are standard clay saucers, but more sophisticated water-catching devices are being developed by manufacturers.

CEILING CONTAINERS
Ceiling containers are the most popular for trailing plants; they come in many materials—wood, plastic, fiber glass, clay—and some

These handsome stainless steel containers can be set on pedestals or suspended with chain from ceilings. (Martin Design Studio photo)

Ceramic tubs and pots are attractive and ornamental; trailing plants are stellar in them. (Author photo)

are more decorative than others. Hanging devices for these containers include chain, rope, raffia, or wire, and ceiling hangers are offered in many styles from gilded screw-in "S" hooks to standard eyebolts and double-duty coffee-cup hangers. The type of hanger and support you choose depends on the weight of the plant and pot. An 8-inch pot filled with soil weighs about 60 pounds—a formidable hazard if it ever slips from its moorings—so buy adequate ceiling hooks and chains.

The shape of the container may be round, elliptical, oval, square, rectangular, or tapered, and selecting the proper design is important. Some plants, such as cascading Petunias and Chrysanthemums, look best in a round pot. Low-growing plants like Sedum and ice plants are handsome in square boxes; Philodendrons, with lance-shaped dark green leaves, are attractive in redwood containers. Other Philodendrons with delicate heart-shaped leaves are better suited to round or oval white pots.

Redwood baskets in many sizes are very popular for trailing plants (Joyce R. Wilson photo)

An appealing architectural planter holds a lacy fern; perfect decoration for any area. (Architectural Pottery Co. photo)

Also consider the material of the container; it should be appropriate with the setting. Wood looks best outdoors, as do terra cotta pots. Indoors, more sophisticated containers such as brass or highly polished silver cylinders may blend more with the interior design. In this case, plants are both green accents and room decoration. Plexiglas boxes and molded glass containers that can be suspended from ceiling hangers are also available and suitable in a contemporary room setting.

Whatever container you select for plants, be sure that it has drainage holes in the bottom (unless it is an open wire or wood basket). If the container is of ceramic or glazed pottery, take it to a glass store and have holes drilled; pots and tubs without drainage facilities are a bother, and watering plants in them requires meticulous care. Generally, in a few months, soil at the bottom becomes soggy and the plants die. However, if you must use tubs and pots without drainage facilities, follow this planting method: put in a 2- to 3- inch bed of gravel or stones (for a 12-inch container) before you add soil. Then excess water will settle in the bottom of the stones and eventually evaporate rather than accumulate in the soil.

The watering schedule for plants also depends on the type of container. For instance, clay pots hold water a short time because the moisture quickly evaporates through the sides. Plastic pots dry out slowly, and plants in them retain moisture over a longer period. This is an advantage to the gardener who is away from home a few days a week. Redwood and wire baskets must be watered daily if plants are to prosper in them, and even though Plexiglas containers are striking in appearance, the material collects algae and must be cleaned frequently. Shallow-hanging dishes are being seen more frequently, but however pretty they may be, they are not for such deep-rooted plants as Clivia or many Philodendrons, since growth is restricted and plants do not prosper. For these containers, select shallow-rooted plants like Bromeliads or Begonias.

Avoid putting small plants in large pots; they will appear out of scale and generally do not grow well because unused soil in the bottom becomes waterlogged. Use a group of small plants if you have a large container. On the other hand, do not set very large plants in small housings, they simply will not have space to grow and eventually will die.

A few years ago, discarded bird cages were seen with trailing plants. The idea was good, but I never really saw a handsome combination of plant and "container." But if you want to try such an arrangement, have a galvanized metal pan made for the bottom of the cage, and be sure to include drainage holes. The pan should be at least 6 inches in depth so that there will be ample soil for small plants. Plant the metal pan as you would a dish garden, and set the cage in place. Provide a strong support; chain is usually the best.

Rattan hangers and containers are pretty and have a tropical appearance. The basket and the support is woven in one piece, and the pot is set in the rattan pouch. Select high-grade rattan; inferior types will deteriorate within 6 months.

When selecting containers for trailing plants, consider these points:
Do the shape and size of the pot blend with the setting?
Does the pot have drainage holes?
Will the plant look good in the container?
Is the container easy to hang?
Will the material last a long time?
Is the container maintenance-free?

WALL AND FLOOR CONTAINERS

Pots for wall mounting are a convenience; they can be placed where you want them, and you do not have to bother with chains and ceiling hooks. The pot is attached with hardware that comes with it, and mounting the pot is generally a matter of putting in a few wall screws. Bracket bowls are handsome and offer the gardener a chance to decorate fences and walls. Some pots mount flat on the wall on a sturdy steel support; others float above an angled steel fixture. Several pot shapes are available, including cylinders, triangular-shaped pots, and convex- or concave-sided rectangles in glazed or unglazed finishes.

Floor-mounted bowls or tubs are also possible containers for trailing plants, presenting an attractive floating-garden effect. These containers are set on metal spikes that are inserted into the ground, thus elevating the planter in mid-air. Indoors the same principle applies, but the bowls have a tripod base.

Wall bracket containers with echeverias add dimension and design to a wall. These young plants have just been started and they eventually will trail over pot edges. (Architectural Pottery Co. photo)

A decorative Mexican pot is home for Campanula. (Author photo)

Here, an unusual container holds cascading ivy and makes a handsome accent on a fence. (Joyce R. Wilson photo)

MAKE YOUR OWN CONTAINERS

Although there are many commercial containers available, you might want to design and make your own for it is inexpensive, and you can put your imagination to work. The most popular do-it-your-self container is the cross-hatched redwood basket, and it can be made in several ways. For example, it can be a box within a box. Select ¾-inch stock for the exterior box, and run 1- x 2-inch lathing horizontally on the outside, spaced ½ inch apart. The strips should be 2 inches longer than the size of the box, with 1 inch overlapping at each end. Or you can build the slotted redwood basket design: the wood strips are notched at each corner and are put together like a log cabin, with each rail notching into the other. Use wood epoxy to seal the joints at the corners. (Drawing #5.)

The cube box is another idea that is neat and simple. For a 2-inch box, 1 x 12-inch rough redwood is best. To give it a finished appearance, stain the wood a darker color and nail 1- x 1-inch strips spaced ⅓ inch apart around it.

The container with flared or tapered sides is handsome and suitable for many different plants. An 18-inch top tapering to a 10-inch base is a good size. Use 1-inch redwood or cedar and miter the corners.

For all custom-made containers, drill holes in the bottom so that excess water can escape. Put small eyelets (two to a side) on the top wooden sections so that there will be places to loop wire or rope.

Wood is the best material, the most popular, and lasts a long time. It is easy to work with, and the natural finish looks good on terraces or patios. Redwood resists rot, weathers beautifully over the years, and needs no outside finish. However, for decorative effect, boxes can be scored, grooved, or sandblasted. Planters are generally nailed together, but glue and wood epoxy last longer. (Use brass screws and high-quality epoxy.)

DRIP-SAUCERS AND OTHER WATER-CATCHING DEVICES

The standard clay saucer is available in many sizes and depths, with a maximum of 20 inches in diameter and 3 inches in depth. Basically, it is set on a flat surface—windowsill or floor—and the container set in the saucer. There are two designs: one with a flared lip and the other plain. For basket containers, the lip-type is neces-

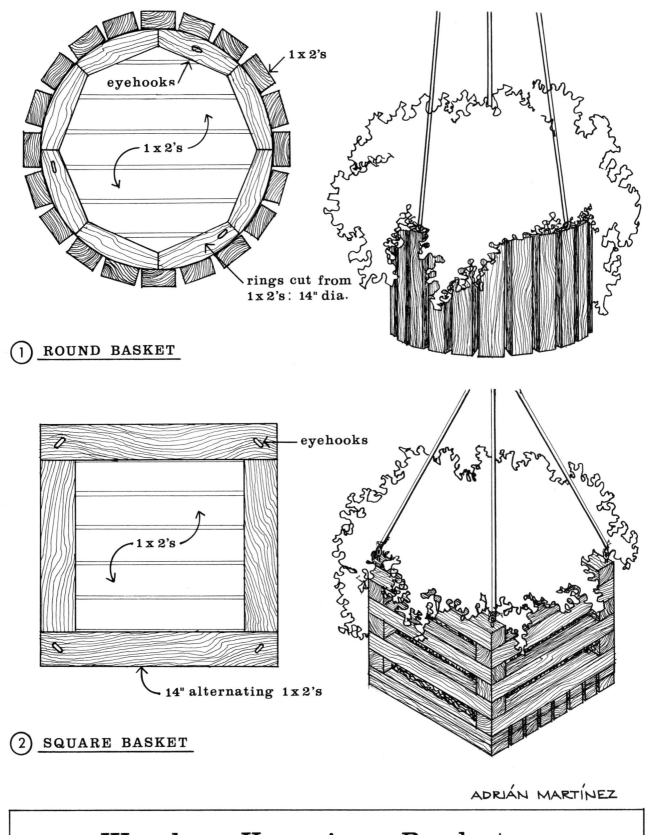

1x2's

eyehooks

1x2's

rings cut from
1x2's: 14" dia.

① __ROUND BASKET__

— eyehooks

1x2's

14" alternating 1x2's

② __SQUARE BASKET__

ADRIÁN MARTÍNEZ

Wooden Hanging Baskets

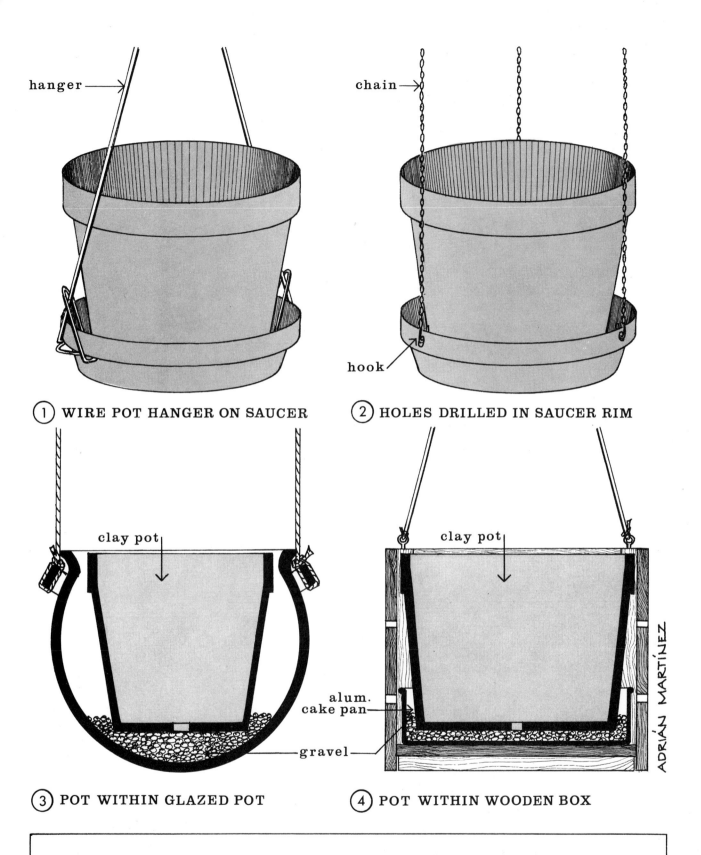

hanger

chain

hook

① WIRE POT HANGER ON SAUCER

② HOLES DRILLED IN SAUCER RIM

clay pot

clay pot

alum.
cake pan

gravel

ADRIÁN MARTÍNEZ

③ POT WITHIN GLAZED POT

④ POT WITHIN WOODEN BOX

Drip Saucers, Water Catching Devices

sary so that pot hangers can grasp its edges and keep the saucer in place under the pot. There are also saucers with wires that attach to the rim of the pot; these have just appeared in nurseries and should be available soon nationwide. Either type will eliminate water stains on floors, but basically they are for standard clay pots and do not fit other containers.

For many pots, tubs, and hanging bowls you will have to make your own drip trays, but this is not difficult. The housewares department of any good store will offer numerous possibilities. Aluminum baking pans of many shapes and sizes are available and can be set in wood frames and attached to pots. (See Drawing #6.) If you would rather not attach the pan to the container, or if it is impossible to do so, pans (filled with gravel to eliminate splashing) can be set directly under the plants on the floor. This is not esthetically pleasing, but it does the job.

Another way to avoid water dripping on floors and furniture is to use a decorative container (without holes) as an outer pot and then slip in the potted plant. This method works well except that the glazed pot will have to be emptied of excess water about once a week.

3. Window Boxes ✐

Window boxes may seem old-fashioned compared with the newly designed hanging containers. Yet there are centuries of tradition behind them, and even though most boxes are planted with upright growers, it is the cascading plants that make them something special. Through the years, the window box has proven itself a good container for plants whether they are used as a seasonal display or for year-round green accent.

Formerly, window boxes were strictly a do-it-yourself project. Now suppliers offer boxes in many materials: wood, plastic, metal, stone, and fiberglass. I have successfully used the green-painted metal ones and the stone type. The plastic and fiberglass containers do not

A bounty of color is harvested in these trailing sweet-peas in redwood boxes.
(Author photo)

have drainage holes, and growing plants in them requires careful watering.

I prefer the wooden box, and since windows vary in size I build my own. It is simple to make, and wood is the best material because it does not overheat in the sun and unlike plastic containers does not hold moisture over a long period. Select redwood or cedar for the box—1 or 2 inches thick—to provide insulation as well as stability. Use brass screws to hold the boards together because nails can be pulled out by warping boards. Drill drain holes ½ inch in diameter in the bottom of the box in order to ensure free drainage of excess water. If you use woods other than redwood or cedar, treat the inside with a preservative (available at hardware stores) to prevent rotting. (Avoid creosote, which can be poisonous to plants.)

If the plain design of the box does not suit the architecture of the house, you can add wood lathing horizontally or vertically to the

Geraniums are especially attractive in window boxes and furnish a great deal of color. (Potted Plant Information Center photo)

front of the box for more detail. Do not make the box too small or too large. Small containers dry out quickly and are out of scale on an average window. Large boxes are cumbersome and heavy when filled with soil, and hanging them properly can become a problem. Thus, two small ones would be better than one very large box. The most satisfactory dimensions for window boxes are 10 inches in width so that there will be ample space for plants, 12 inches in depth so that there will be room for enough soil for plant roots, and 30 to 36 inches in length.

Window boxes filled with soil are heavy and must be securely fastened to the building wall; bolt them to wall studs or fasten them with lag screws. Remember: a 4-foot box filled with soil weighs about

300 pounds! Leave some space between the box and wall for the movement of air. On solid surfaces, raise boxes on wood cleats or bricks so that drainage holes won't become clogged. For safety I also install a pair of sturdy L-shaped iron brackets to support the boxes.

In regions with freezing winters, boxes must be emptied of soil and covered with plastic to prevent them from cracking. This can be a troublesome chore; removing pounds of soil takes several hours (I know because I have done it). To avoid this situation, do not pot directly into the box; merely set potted plants inside it and fill in and around the pots with sphagnum. It is easy then to move plants into the house in cold weather, and it is not necessary to buy soil every year.

The idea of window-box gardening is a sound one. Plants benefit from rain and are exposed to the circulation of air on all sides. Soil dries out rapidly in window boxes; water plants frequently and thoroughly until excess water runs out of the bottom of the box. Flowering plants such as Petunia and Lantana will often need water twice a day in hot weather.

To prepare the box for planting, put in a layer of pot shards or gravel; then put in a bed of soil and position plants. Fill in and around the plants with soil. Leave at least 1 inch at the top of the box so that it will be easy to water the soil. A good window-box soil consists of 2 parts garden loam, 1 part leaf mold, 1 part peat moss, and 1 part sharp sand.

An attractive variation of the window-box idea is shelves—wide boards with holes to support pots at the rim. The rim of the pot rests on the edge of the hole; this is a window box without the box. This kind of window-box is especially handsome for cottage-type windows.

Window-Box Plants for Shade or Partial Shade (For description, see Chapter 7)

Achimenes	Ferns
Aeschynanthus lobbianus	Fuchsias
Coleus (trailing type)	*Hedera helix*
Campanula	*Tradescantia blossfeldiana*
Episcia	Tuberous Begonias (Pendula type)

In vertical wooden window box, these succulents will soon create a tapestry of green. (Author photo)

Window-Box Plants for Sun

Bougainvillea
Cobaea scandens
Ivy Geraniums
Lantana montevidensis

Lobelia
Petunias (cascading varieties)
Thunbergia alata
Tropaeolum (nasturtium)

VERTICAL GARDENS

The vertical garden is a somewhat modified window box with a vertical rather than a horizontal growing surface. It is a unique way to decorate a railing or fence with flower and foliage. These boxes are almost exclusively for hanging plants, although I have grown small creeping succulents in them with great success.

The boxes are hung like pictures on a wall, and a wire mesh screening on the face of the box is inner-lined with sphagnum moss to hold in soil and plants. Do not use close-mesh wire; there must be room between the wires for plants. Use small boxes rather than cumbersome large ones. An ideal size is 16 x 30 inches in length and 12 inches in depth.

Succulent plants grow lavishly in a vertical wooden window box. (Author photo)

To plant the box place it flat on a table, and work in plants between the wires. For a few weeks, until soil and plants settle, do not hang the box; keep it in a somewhat shady and warm place. Once plants are established the vertical garden can be hung.

4. Plant Stands for Trailing Plants ☞

We usually see trailing plants in suspended containers, but they can be lovely in other situations too. They are well suited to plant stands and pedestals; their trailing columns of foliage balance the vertical design of the stand. They are equally handsome on shelves or wrought iron credenzas because the cascading foliage softens the lines of corners and does not leave corners and hardware exposed.

PLANT STANDS

Some stands are made of wood; others are made of wrought iron or aluminum. Design varies, but generally the stand has a central post with adjustable arms that can be moved in a circle, with drip-saucer holders welded to the arms. Some stands accommodate as many as sixteen plants, and these are ideal for the apartment dweller with little space. It is possible to have a beautiful pot garden in a small area.

Use both upright and trailing plants for stands so that there is vertical accent as well as mass. Position the holders (if they are adjustable) so that they are not directly above each other; dripping water on crowns of plants can produce rot. Most stands are 48 to 60 inches high, and the holders are about 6 inches in diameter; thus, massive plants cannot be used so select choice species of small- and medium-sized growers.

The plant stand, like the basket container, is a display area for plants so keep them well groomed: trim errant growth, and pick off faded blossoms immediately. Choose stands with care; some are ill balanced and can be knocked over easily.

PEDESTAL STANDS AND POTS

The pedestal that accommodates one plant is usually made of wood, ornate, and expensive; recently some moderate-priced reproductions have appeared at suppliers. The pedestals vary from 3 to 7 feet in height. Most are impressive pieces of furniture, so the plants for them must be lush and dramatic. Choose specimen plants that will be in scale to the pedestal. Ferns are excellent candidates, as are some of the large Begonias.

Architectural pottery serves as another container for trailing plants. Of contemporary design, these tubs and pots gracefully elevate the plant and come in a variety of bowls fused on clay- or vinyl-covered bases of varying height. They can be placed almost anywhere in a room for a spot of color, so trailing plants or those with rosette growth are excellent on them.

Similar in concept but different in design are tubs set in wooden

An iron plant-stand in the corner of a garden room furnishes space for several trailing plants. (Author photo)

Wooden shelves with handsome trailing
plants become a partition of a room.
(Potted Plant Info. Center photo)

Pedestal rattan stands hold grape-ivy;
a smart decoration for this area.
(McGuire Furniture Photo)

rails or metal pipes. The container is held in place by the supports. These stands elevate plants about 8 to 12 inches from the floor.

SHELVES

Contemporary metal-and-plexiglas shelves are other good places for graceful pendant growers. These are used as dividers or bookcases: full trailing plants at the corners of shelves add lovely green accent and cover any exposed hardware. Do not use too many plants to a unit; only a few are necessary for accent.

For a very decorative garden, old-fashioned bakers' platforms are available; the wrought-iron bars are 3 to 4 inches apart, and there are generally three shelves. Originally used for cooling bread, these platforms are handsome accents with trailing plants against a decorative wrought-iron trellis. The genuine bakers' shelves are scarce and expensive, but reproductions are now available from furniture outlets.

Plants for Pedestals (For description, see Chapter 7)

Angel-wing Begonias	*Clerodendrum thomsoniae*
Asparagus sprengeri	Coleus (trailing varieties)
Begonia 'Cleopatra'	*Medinella magnifica*
Chlorophytum elatum	

Plants for Shelves

Aesychananthus lobbianus	*Hypocyrta strigillosa*
Columnea	Petunias
Hedera helix	*Rhipsalis paradoxa*
Hoya carnosa	

Plants for Stands

Cissus	Syngonium
Episcia	*Tolmiea menziesii*
Hedera helix	Tradescantia
Hoya carnosa	Zebrina
Saxifraga sarmentosa	

5. Indoors and Outdoors with Basket Plants ☞

Today, living plants are an essential part of the indoor scene. We use them as structural elements in the total design. Because they become part of the room, choose plants with care. Some trailers are delicate and lacy; others bold and heavy in appearance. The plant must suit the interior and at the same time be in scale to the other objects in the room. A large *Asparagus sprengeri* crammed against a wall or placed in a small room is simply not handsome.

For small places where you want a cottage effect, use small-leaved plants such as *Ficus pumila* and *Hoya carnosa*. In a large contemporary area, Orchids or a large-leaved Philodendron are suitable. For a touch of drama in a room try such exotic flowering plants as Epiphyllums (Orchid cactus).

Outdoors, bright colorful baskets of plants are instant decoration and transform any area into a special place. There is no need to go through the hard work of digging out soil or to worry about the soil being able to support plants. In a few hours, a barren patio can become a tropical greenery with basket plants.

In Living and Dining Rooms
Eye-level gardens add vertical accent to a room and are used like pictures on a wall. Especially in corners or in a stairwell, they can be a valuable asset to the total décor. Do not hang them too high or too low. (See Drawing #7.)

If there is space, use more than one plant; three pots at different heights create a handsome effect. If plants are small, try the fountain-tier arrangement—three plants—one under the other in a col-

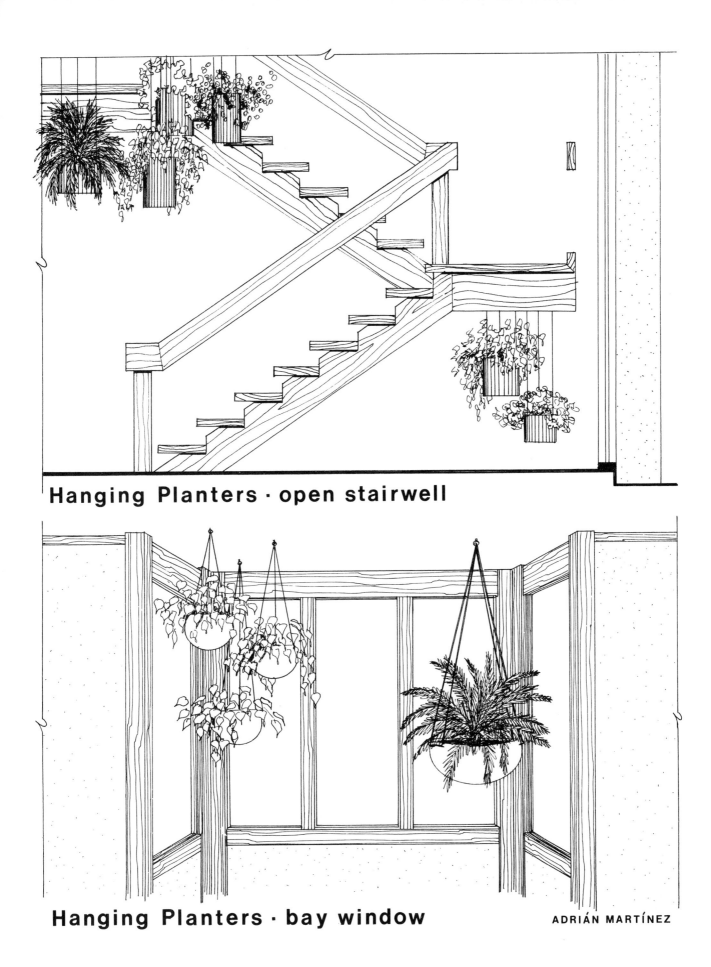

Hanging Planters · open stairwell

Hanging Planters · bay window

ADRIÁN MARTÍNEZ

Left: *Grape ivy in a handsome ceramic container adds charm to a dining room corner.* (Joyce R. Wilson photo)

Right: *A kitchen window is a perfect place for the Lipstick-vine (Aeschynanthus).* (Author photo)

umn. To achieve this effect, suspend the first plant from the ceiling, then hook the hanger of the second pot into the drain hole of the first pot and the hanger of the third pot into the drain hole of the second pot. This creates a column of green rather than a solitary spot of color. (See Drawing #8.)

If plants cannot be near windows, select species that will tolerate shade. Philodendron, grape ivy, and many Ferns are good candidates for such places. Flowering plants need all the light they can get or else bloom will be sparse, if at all.

Shape and prune plants so that they are sculptural elements against walls. Do not be afraid to cut straggly branches or ill-shaped growth; this is the only way to have a handsome eye-appealing plant.

Chose indoor containers (shape, design, and material) to complement other objects in the room. If the budget will allow, use handsome stainless steel, aluminum, or brass containers, or some of the new and attractive leather-faced tubs, thus making the plant and its container an attractive part of the room. Avoid clay, plastic, and wooden pots indoors for usually they appear out of place. These materials are better suited to the outdoor scene where they blend in with the surroundings.

Left: *In a standard clay pot, grape-ivy is the vertical accent in a stairwell. Note attached drip-saucer.* (Joyce R. Wilson photo)

Right: *Sedum morganianum (Burro's tail) is a feature of a patio; it is a rainbow of color in summer with apple-green stems and pale pink flowers. The hidden container is a large redwood basket.* (Joyce R. Wilson photo)

FOR PATIO AND TERRACE

There is a wide choice of plants and containers for outdoor decoration. Redwood baskets and terra cotta pots are handsome, and almost any flowering trailer can be grown in them. Columneas with bright tubular blooms and Orchids with dramatic flowers are especially desirable as are Dipladenias and Clerodendrums.

With a few exceptions, most flowering plants will need sun. Hang them at the same height from porch rafters; use three or four (rather than a solitary plant) in a row equi-distant from each other. You may also group three pots at different heights in one area in which case do not hang plants too high; place them at eye level so that watering is no problem. At the same time, be sure that they are out of the path of traffic; it is bothersome to have to duck under potted plants.

Wall containers hold Chlorophytum seedlings; in a few months the pendent leaves will cover the pots. (Architectural Pottery Photo)

Outdoors, plants dry out quickly and in hot weather may need water twice a day. Keep the soil evenly moist, and feed plants with a soluble fertilizer (see Chapter 6) about twice a month. Occasionally wash leaves with a strong spray of water to eliminate insects and dust.

If the outdoor area does not have an overhang or eaves to hang plants, install wall brackets. These wrought-iron holders (available at suppliers) are a continuous piece of iron with a ring device; merely slip pots in place. Once again, do not use a solitary plant against a wall. Instead, put three of them one under the other for a wall of color. Or make your own wall mounted planters. (See Drawing #8).

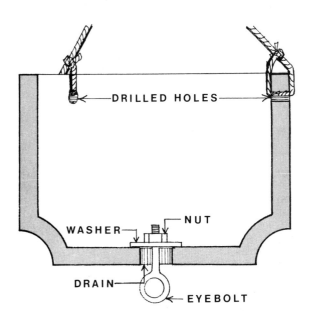

DRILLED HOLES

WASHER — NUT

DRAIN —

— EYEBOLT

Hanging Planters · tiered

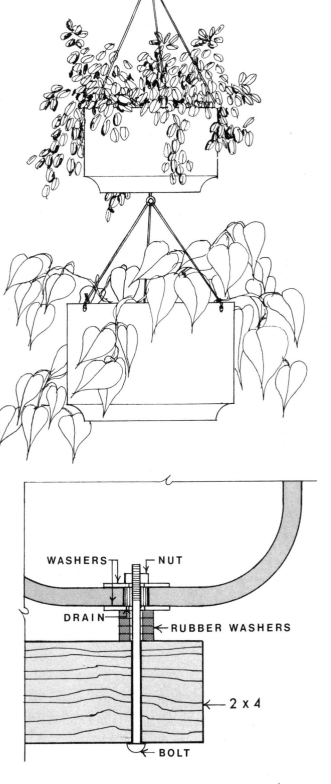

WASHERS — NUT

DRAIN —

— RUBBER WASHERS

← 2 x 4

← BOLT

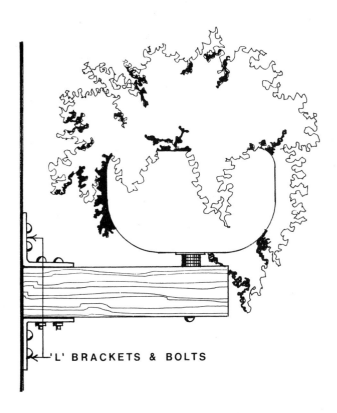

'L' BRACKETS & BOLTS

Planter · wall mounted

ADRIÁN MARTÍNEZ

6. Keeping Plants Healthy ✑

Once plants are in place indoors or on patio and terrace, keep them handsome so that they are attractive additions to the area. This means giving them a certain amount of attention; some plants are difficult to grow, most are not.

Generally, basket plants need either cool growing conditions or warmth. Cool-growing plants will respond to average home temperatures, that is, 68 to 78° F during the day and 10 to 15 degrees lower at night. Warm-growing plants need a higher night temperature; about 55 to 60°F. will suit most of them, but there is no need to adjust your heating to the plant's needs. Instead, there are always places in the home where it is a little cooler or warmer than in other areas: an unheated but not freezing sunporch or spare room would be ideal for cool-growing plants.

For most plants, average house humidity or air moisture of 30 to 40 percent is adequate. There are very few plants discussed in this book that would need more humidity, and these exceptions can be accommodated in various ways. Misting with a spray gun a few times a day or providing pebble trays for plants helps to increase humidity. Fresh air is also essential if you want healthy plants. Even in cold weather try to keep a window open in the growing area; however, be sure plants are not in direct drafts as this will harm them.

SOIL AND REPOTTING
A good potting soil contains enough adequate nutrients to carry a plant through a least one growing season. Avoid repotting plants frequently; it disturbs the lush beauty that is the charm of baskets.

A Coleus is well-grown with plenty of light and ample moisture. (Joyce R. Wilson photo)

For most plants, use 1 part garden loam to 1 part sand to 1 part leaf mold. For Cacti and some Succulents, alow more sand, and for acid-loving plants such as Azaleas and Tuberous Begonias add a handful of peat moss to each 8-inch pot. If you do not have time to mix your own soil, buy it from a local greenhouse or nursery; it is the same soil they use. It has been sterilized and contains all necessary ingredients and you can use it as it is for almost all plants.

Such epiphytic hanging plants as some Orchids, Bromeliads, and Christmas and Easter Cacti are best grown in fir bark or osmunda fiber. These materials are in packages at most nurseries.

"Soiless" mixes are also available from suppliers. These are light-weight and inexpensive but contain no nutrients so plants growing in it must be fed year-round, and this becomes a chore. When you purchase soil, ask the nurseryman about it; it should contain humus and leaf mold, be porous, and yet drain readily.

Many times you will buy potted plants ready for hanging. Other times you will want to put plants in new containers. The sooner you repot, the sooner the plant will become established to make a colorful display. Most plants can be repotted in any season except winter. Try to remove the rootball intact from the old container. Do not pull

This hanging plant is in a poor location without ample light to sustain growth.
(Joyce R. Wilson photo)

or tug it; rather, jiggle it loose from the pot. Then crumble some of
the old soil from the roots, and place it in a new container with fresh
soil. Set the plant in a bright place without sunlight for a few days,
and then assign it to its permanent place. Do not panic if the plant
loses a few leaves or appears wilted after repotting. This is a natural
condition until the plant becomes adjusted to a new situation.

All plants need light to grow and there are plants for all exposures,
including north-shade windows. Choose plants for the conditions
you can give them. A Fern will not respond in bright sunlight and a

sun lover such as Achimenes will not thrive in shade. The brightest light is near a window, and at 5 feet from the glass, light is greatly diminished.

Light intensity changes with the seasons. In summer light is at its brightest, and some plants will need shading at windows; a screen does the job. In winter, the sun is at a different angle in the sky and light is weaker.

Turn plants occasionally so light reaches all sides of the foliage.

WATERING AND FEEDING

If you are accustomed to growing window plants, you will find that the watering schedule for basket plants is different. With air circulating around the container and where light is available from all sides, plants dry out quickly, especially those in wire or open-sided containers. During the warm months, plants may have to be watered daily and in fall and winter, depending upon artificial heat, perhaps every other day.

When you water do it thoroughly, so that excess water pours from the drainage hole and the complete root system gets moisture. If only the top soil gets wet and the lower parts stays dry, the growth of the plant is retarded. Water at room temperature is best, and if possible, water in the morning, so that the soil can dry out before dark. Lingering moisture and cool nights are an invitation to fungus disease.

Many plants benefit from feeding; however, Orchids, Clerodendrum, and some other flowering plants do not need it. Commercial fertilizers contain a good part of nitrogen which stimulates foliage growth, but too much of it can hinder development of flower buds. The ratio of elements is marked on the bottle or package in this order: nitrogen, phosphorous, and potash. There are many formulas, and I find 10-10-5 the best for most plants.

PLANT PROTECTION

Plants that are directly in the ground or in pots at ground level may be plagued with crawling insects, but hanging baskets are rarely affected. It is seldom necessary to use strong insecticides when you grow basket plants. Keep your plants well-groomed; pick off faded flowers and dead leaves, and wipe or mist foliage with clear tepid water about once a week. This cleansing will remove insect eggs and spider mites and in general discourages pests.

Many times, a plant does not respond because of poor culture. Falling leaves and premature bud-drop are not necessarily caused by insects or disease. Before you resort to chemical warfare consider these cultural points:

Is the humidity too high or too low for plants?
Are there drafts in the growing area?
Has the soil become sour from overwatering?
Is the plant getting enough light—or too much?
Have there been sudden changes in temperature?
Have you been using icy water for plants?

If all the cultural aspects are good and the plant still declines, check for insects or diseases. Most of the common plant insects such as mealybugs and aphids can be seen; evidence of spider mites can be seen as webs at the plant's leaf axils. Scale, an insect with a hard or soft shell, also can be seen, and slugs or snails are easily recognized.

Even when you see pests on your plants do not rush for chemicals. Some good home remedies are a better procedure. A thorough washing at the sink often eliminates aphids; a solution of a tablespoon of alcohol to a quart of laundry-soap water will do the job too. Scale can be removed with a stiff brush dipped in soapy water, and this same solution will deter red spiders. Potatoes cut in half and placed on the soil will lure snails and sow bugs to the surface where you can destroy them. Beer does the job, too.

Even with the best of culture, occasionally a plant will suffer insect attack. If you do not want to use home remedies select one of the safer nonpersistent insecticides: Diazinon, Malathion, or Sevin. When using chemicals follow the manufacturers' directions to the letter, and keep all products out of the reach of children and pets. I store chemicals in an old medicine chest in the garage; it is high on the wall where children can not reach it.

Bacterial diseases such as mildew and botrytis might occasionally attack a plant. A sign of mildew is leaves that are coated white; botrytis can be seen as gray mold on flowers and leaves. Fungicides such as Zineb or Phaltan are recommended by most gardeners for these diseases. However, I do not like to use poisons in the home and

Well grown plants are rarely attacked by insects; these plants are in suspended hanging garden containers from Architectural Pottery Co. (Architectural Pottery Photo)

I usually discard the plant unless it is a rare species or one that I am especially fond of.

SEASONAL CARE

A controlling factor for plant growth indoors and outdoors is the cycle of the year. As seasons change, so do plant requirements. New growth begins in spring, and March and April can be the busiest months for the gardener starting new plants and refurbishing old ones. Make sure the plants are ready for the warming trend; new soil with adequate nutrients starts them off right.

In summer, with the additional light and warmth, most plants grow rapidly, and some, such as Fuchsias and Columneas, may need water twice a day. Now is the time to give weak feeding to plants every other watering. Also, protect plants from the noonday sunlight, which will be too strong now for most of them. Usually a thin curtain or a window screen is all that is required. Avoid a stuffy atmosphere so that pests and insects do not have a chance to gather. On very hot days, mist plants several times to reduce the heat. (Exceptions would be hairy-leaved plants which do not like moisture on their leaves.)

Fall brings changing weather: some hot days and some cool days. It is a crucial time for basket plants. Water them with care; it is better to carry them a little dry into winter rather than having them too moist. Stop feeding, and in winter, when few plants are in active growth, keep soil barely moist.

7. Trailing and Hanging Plants 🍃

Although there are true trailing and hanging plants, such as Tuberous Begonias, Fuchsias and ivy Geraniums, other plants can be grown in baskets. Some are more appropriate than others; that is, they have dense foliage and grow quickly enough to fill a basket in a short time. Others, such as Ceropegia or Abutilon (although always classified as hanging plants), are generally straggly and ill-suited for baskets.

Ferns, not often thought of as basket plants, are at their best at eye level, where their arching fronds can be fully appreciated, rather than placed at windows or shelves. Many fine species are available: some have feathery fronds, and others, such as Cyrtomium, have wide, dark green leaflets.

Succulents, an overlooked group of plants, offer many fine candidates for basket growing and include Aeoniums, with clusters of handsome rosettes, Kleinias, with cascading pencils of blue, Crassulas, Sedums, and Kalanchoes. Philodendron, Chlorophytum, and Peperomia are other good plants for basket growing.

There are a host of annuals and bulbs that are lovely when grown in baskets: Browallia, Coleus, Impatiens, Lantana, Oxalis, and Vinca.

A lush Fern accents a patio area. (Hort Pix photo)

There are hundreds of plants to grow for almost any situation. Even Caladiums and Dieffenbachias can take to the air with advantage.

For simplification, we have classified plants as either foliage or flowering kinds. Also included is a special list on favorites such as Philodendron, Ferns, Gesneriads, Succulents, Orchids and Bromeliads.

Generally, foliage plants are for indoors but can also be used for patio and terrace decoration. The flowering species which demand sun are mostly seen outdoors but can—during their blooming season —be used in the home, too.

FOLIAGE PLANTS

Rheo (Moses-in-the-cradle)

Not really a trailer but a handsome easy to grow plant from Mexico and the West Indies with rosettes of stiff dark green almost black leaves, purple underneath. The beauty of the plant is its spreading habit and lush growth; it soon fills the container. Keep the soil evenly moist all year. *R. discolor* is the popular species.

Cissus

These relatives of the grape family are excellent indoors where tough plants are needed. They survive untoward conditions for months and still remain beautiful. The best one is *C. rhombifolia* (grape ivy) which has glossy, toothed-and-pointed leaves. It will climb if you furnish support (string will do), or it will cascade over the pot rim. *C. antarctica,* (the kangaroo vine) is another fine species for baskets. It has long narrow leaves, and is brown-veined, dark green and toothed; it needs little care. If more color is wanted, try *C. discolor.* It has lovely heart-shaped, velvety green leaves marked with pink or purple. This one needs more warmth and humidity than the others.

These plants are fast growers. Start two or three of them in a 6-inch pot; within a year they will fill the container.

Asparagus sprengeri (asparagus fern)

Two kinds of asparagus plants have been favorites for a long time but only recently have become appreciated. *A. plumosus* is a true climber; *A. sprengeri* (the emerald fern) has arching fronds of feathery green. Either one is a stalwart performer in a basket.

Asparagus ferns usually send out nonclimbing growths before they are old enough to climb. Then once established they will grow quickly. *A. sprengeri* has rich green and needlelike foliage. Mature plants will bear fragrant white flowers followed by red berries in winter.

Within a year, either plant will fill an 8-inch pot. They need ample space, for they grow quite large, and plenty of water and a bright place to thrive. These ferns are highly desirable pot plants suspended from chains in stairwells or in room corners.

Hedera helix (English ivy)

Scores of superb Ivies with exquisite foliage are at nurseries. Some have dark green leaves; others are variegated. Because of their airy quality they are handsome plants, but they do have some stringent requirements. Most of them need coolness (about 58°F at night) and are subject to attack by spider mites.

Spray plants frequently with water in hot weather, and inspect them monthly for insect attack. Grow several plants in a container for a good display, and be ruthless about pruning them to shape. If you let them grow naturally, they can become straggly. Some fine varieties to try are 'Goldheart,' and 'Fan.'

Hoya carnosa (wax-plant)

This plant has been popular for years. Mature specimens are a spectacle with handsome, fragant, waxlike flowers and gray-green oval leaves. The wax-plant climbs and trails, so provide suitable support. After blossoms fade, do not remove flower spurs; subsequent flowers can come from the same spurs.

H. carnosa is not a fast-growing plant, and it takes several years before it is really attractive. Young plants are difficult to start, so select mature ones. Grow them somewhat cool (58°F at night) with bright light. Too much water will kill them.

Scindapsus aureus (ivy-arum)

This fine plant and its many varieties make stellar basket gardens. The original species *S. aureus* has heart-shaped dark green leaves marked with yellow marbling. Many varieties have smaller leaves, some with pure white markings. Others come in various shades of cream or yellow and include 'Silver Moon,' 'Tricolor,' 'Marble Queen,' and 'Arum Ivy,' to name a few. Although the plants grow large they never make a spectacular show, but they do have definite charm.

Scindapsus plants are easy to grow; give them average light, and allow soil to dry out between waterings. Shape them by cutting off leaves when necessary so that the plants become bushy.

Chlorophytum (spider-plant)

These overlooked plants offer foolproof color for indoors or outdoors. They grow as easily as weeds, and with their graceful grassy

Hedera helix

Hoya carnosa exotica

leaves they make a lovely display within a year. Plants have storage tubers for water, so if you forget to water them for a few days they do not suffer. Plantlets are produced at the end of flower stalks and are graceful pendants, appearing like green shooting stars in mid-air.

There are varieties with white or cream markings on green leaves, (*C. elatum variegatum*) but these are somewhat more difficult to grow than the plain green type called *C. elatum*. All varieties need bright light and buckets of water during the warm months but not so much the rest of the year. Don't miss this group of plants; it is a lot of greenery for little money.

Coleus

Usually considered a summer bedding plant rather than a basket plant, Coleus varieties have colorful foliage that is just too good to miss. Red and purple leaves predominate, but I prefer the apple-green and yellow varieties, There are trailers, such as *C. rehneltianus* and its varieties, or upright types such as *C. blumei*.

Grow Coleus plants in a sunny or bright location, keep them warm and evenly moist all year, and inspect foliage for spider mites.

Syngonium (Nephthytis)

It is a pity that these plants do not have a common name, for surely the botanical name dissuades people from growing them. Although not glamorous or outstanding in color, Syngoniums nevertheless have decorative leaf shapes ranging from a simple arrowhead design to unequal-sized segments. Foliage leaf color is outstanding; many are colorfully variegated with yellow, chartreuse, white, or silver markings.

These plants are upright climbers, and without a support they become graceful trailing plants that do not grow too rapidly. Give them bright light, keep the soil evenly moist at all times, and water often.

Saxifraga sarmentosa (strawberry geranium)

These are neither Strawberries, Geraniums, nor Begonias, but actually members of the Saxifragaceae, of which the Hydrangea is a member. The strawberry part of the name has evolved because the plant sends out runners from a clump of basal leaves, and it is these runners that make the plant effective for hanging. *S. sarmentosa*,

Chlorophytum elatum variegatum

with soft, round, hairy leaves, purple underneath, is the most popular in the group. It is pretty, but these are small plants, never really showy.

Saxifragas dislike strong sunlight and are at their best in shade. Keep them moist, but occasionally let them dry out between waterings. They are charming for the hanging garden with limited space.

Tolmiea menziesii (piggyback plant)

This is a curious plant that has thin light green leaves with plantlets at the base of the mature leaves. Large plants are indeed attractive with long-leaf petioles cascading over the pot rim. The open rosette growth is handsome, and this plant thrives in coolness (say 50°F) where other plants might not succeed.

Keep Tolmiea in a bright location, and soil should be evenly moist throughout the year. Not usually classified for basket growing, Tolmiea is nevertheless very effective in such a situation.

Zebrina (wandering jew)

Here is a plant that will grow in almost any situation and in any soil. With thickened trailing stems and glistening foliage striped with silver, pink, or white, Zebrina has long oval leaves that grow rapidly, and plants soon fill a basket. It can become straggly in appearance, so pinch off leaves when necessary to create an attractive shape.

Tradescantia (wandering jew)

Similar to Zebrina and often confused with it, some of these plants have large blue-green leaves others, green and white foliage. *T. fluminensis* is the species most often seen, but *T. blossfeldiana*, with a reddish purple color, is more suitable for hanging baskets. Plants need some sunlight and coolness; keep soil evenly moist. Plants are intolerant of drafts and fluctuating temperatures.

Myrsine nummularia

This is a miniature plant with buttonlike glossy green leaves on wiry stems. It never grows too large and is ideal where a small spot of color is needed. Grow several plants to a container. Culture is simple: bright light and ample moisture throughout the year. Not an outstanding plant, but it is charming.

Tolmiea menziesii

Tradescantia fluminensis

Gelsimium sempervirens (Carolina-jessamine)

A choice twining shrub to about 40 inches with ornamental shiny green leaves, and sometimes funnel-shaped yellow flowers that are deliciously fragrant. Try it for scent if nothing else.

Ficus pumila (repens) (creeping fig)

Never spectacular but always desirable is this fine creeping plant with tiny 1-inch leaves. It grows into a dense ball of color if given plenty of water and a well-ventilated location.

Gynura aurantiaca (velvet-plant)

With purple leaves, this plant glows with color in good light. It adapts well to basket growing and becomes a lush display. Keep soil evenly moist. Fine indoor accent for eye-level gardens.

FLOWERING PLANTS

Lantana montevidensis

In a hanging container Lantana is a beautiful display with its cascading green foliage and superb clusters of lavender flowers. Some time during the year give it a short rest as it might bloom itself to death. Curtail watering for about a month. Pinch back frequently to shape the plant. Grow in a sunny place, mist foliage frequently, and let soil dry out between waterings.

Petunias

Everyone is familiar with these grand flowers, and the cascading varieties are stunning in bloom in midsummer. Pots overflow with blossoms and these are hard plants to resist. Many colors are available, but to me the deep red varieties are the prettiest. Buy them at local nurseries, and grow three or four to a 8-inch pot. Give Petunias plenty of sunlight and water. Start new plants yearly.

Impatiens

These are rarely considered basket plants, but they certainly are at their best in a hanging garden. Select the small-leaved variety called 'Elfin.' It is floriferous, and a well-grown plant will be a cloud of

Cherry Blossom petunias are pictured here in a bird cage suspended with chains from a ceiling. (Pan American Seed Co. photo)

Baskets of trailing Petunias add color to this outdoor scene. (Pan American Seed Co. photo)

color. Keep the plant in a bright place (sunlight is not necessary), pinch back occasionally to ensure bushiness, and always give Impatiens plenty of water. Let plant die back in fall; leave it in its pot and store over winter. Start new plants in new soil in spring. Impatiens give an outstanding bounty of flowers even for the novice gardener.

Chrysanthemums

Chrysanthemums make spectacular baskets of color, but they are difficult to train and must be bought mature at local florists. Even though they last only about 6 weeks, the display is worth the expenditure. Give them plenty of water and sunlight, and they will bloom continuously for many weeks. You can try to cut them back after blooming and start them again in a few weeks, but this has never worked for me.

Browallia speciosa

This is an outdoor plant that occasionally will adapt to indoor conditions. It gives a bounty of white-throated violet flowers and makes a splendid hanging garden. It needs sun, coolness, and an airy situation.

Abutilon hybridum (flowering maple)

A flowering plant with hollyhock-type flowers in many colors, Abutilon is difficult to grow but handsome. These plants have maple-shaped leaves and colorful blossoms through spring and summer. They grow rapidly and need shifting from one pot to another as they develop. When the plant is in a 10-inch pot, set it in its permanent place, and allow it to become pot-bound for maximum bloom. Trim occasionally or else it will become straggly. *A. megapotamicum variegatum* has green and yellow leaves.

Give flowering maples sun, and keep the soil adequately moist in the warm months or they will quickly wilt. Take cuttings when the plant has spent itself, usually in a year or so, and start fresh.

Campanula

From the bellflower family comes Campanula. It has handsome colorful flowers—blue or white—that make for desirable basket

Cascading Petunia

Impatiens – dwarf

subjects. There are several varieties that have single or double flowers in white, blue, or intense blue. The most popular perhaps are *C. fragilis* (purplish blue) and *C. isophylla* (light blue). Campanulas are small- to medium-sized plants and never grow to large proportions, so they are ideal for limited space.

Thse plants need some sun and rather cool temperatures, about 70°F. Keep them well watered in spring and summer and somewhat on the dry side the rest of year. Start several plants in a basket until they become established, and don't expect overnight success.

Dipladenia amoena (Mexican love vine)

Also sold under the name Mandevilla, this is a real stunner similar to a morning glory, that offers a bounty of bright rose-pink flowers. Blooms last for 3 or 4 days and continue, one following the other, for several months. The crinkled green leaves are also attractive and a perfect foil for the lovely flowers. Plants grow quickly and become a desirable addition to the hanging garden.

Give Dipladenia plenty of water in the warm months and not so much the rest of the year. Keep it in the sun, and spray occasionally with water.

Clerodendrum thompsoniae (glory-bower)

There are many fine Clerodendrums, and *C. thomsoniae*, is the best one for baskets. It has beautiful crimson flowers with pure white calyx and lovely green leaves. Plants need ample space for they can, within a season, grow very large. A mature specimen will bloom twice, once in spring and again in late summer. An easy plant to grow, Clerodendrum deserves more attention from gardeners.

Plants need a bright location; a west exposure is fine. Keep soil evenly moist all year.

Medinilla magnifica

A big plant with large leaves and penduluos pink flowers that resemble wisteria, Medinilla can grow very large, so it will need ample support in a basket. It is slow to establish itself and can be quite difficult through its youth, but it can, with care, become a handsome display plant.

Give Medinilla a bright spot, and let the soil dry out between waterings.

Abutilon megapotamicum variegatum

Campanula isophylla

Bougainvillea (paper flower)

A lovely popular vine that is exquisite in summer with bright red or orange bracts and dark green leaves. The orange variety is somewhat difficult to grow so ask for Bougainvillea 'Barbara Karst' or B. 'San Diego Red'. Plants need bright sun to prosper and buckets of water; not so much moisture in winter when they rest. You will have to train plants to basket growing; clip and cut as necessary.

Ruellia makoyana

A charming plant that gives much color for little effort. It has silver-veined leaves and red flowers. Keep soil barely moist; Ruellia is quite sensitive to overwatering. This is one is always welcome in the hanging garden.

Stephanotis floribunda (Madagascar-jasmine)

If you are a good gardener, don't miss Stephanotis for flower and fragrance. The blooms are waxy white, a handsome foil for the dark green leathery leaves. Plants need frequent misting to keep them healthy, and water about three times a week. Temperamental, but worth the challenge.

Beloperone guttata (shrimp-plant)

Here is an old favorite that rarely fails to please. It will clamber and climb all over a container and eventually make a lovely show. The shrimp-plant has coral-colored bracts and deep green leaves. Allow it to dry out between waterings.

Cestrum parqui (willow-leaved jessamine)

A rambler rather than a trailer, this heavenly-scented jessamine is quite suitable for baskets. It has greenish-white flowers and needs pruning to keep it in bounds. Give it plenty of water and a cool place.

Manettia bicolor (mexican-firecracker)

Rarely seen but worth the search is this climbing plant from Brazil. It has tubular yellow-tipped flowers almost all year in a sunny place. Manettia thrives when potbound and requires an airy location. Let soil dry out between waterings.

Mahernia verticillata (honeyballs)

A rangy plant but with charm, and the fragrant yellow flowers are welcome in spring. It is a good basket plant: soak soil and let dry before watering again.

Passiflora caerulea (passion-vine)

A handsome Brazilian vine but really a difficult plant to grow unless you are a superb gardener. The summer or fall flowers are stunning; they are dark blue-and-pink. Flood plants in summer and rest them almost dry for about three months after they bloom. Makes a lovely display in a white tub.

SOME POPULAR PLANT FAMILIES

Through the years some plant families become more popular than others. There may be plants in the group that are easy to grow or have some outstanding character or have been more readily available than other plants. Gesneriads and Ferns are in this group; so are Philodendrons, a long-time favorite.

Many conservatory plants such as Orchids and Bromeliads have been a huge success indoors, too. And Succulents, always reliable standbys are also included in the following list.

GESNERIADS

This flowering family of plants which includes African violets has many noteworthy trailers: Columnea, Episcia, Aesychnanthus, Kohleria, Hypocyrta, and Achimenes. These are bright colorful plants with pendent growth. For all their beauty, they are not difficult to grow but do require more care than foliage plants. Generally, they need a great deal of heat and humidity during the summer when many of them are in bloom. In winter, they can be grown somewhat dry and in a shady location.

Start big pots of Gesneriads because as a rule they do not like to be disturbed; repotting sets them back considerably. It takes a plant about 6 months to become established, so do not be concerned if there are no flowers the first year.

Columneas from tropical America have small opposite leaves and large, tubular, showy flowers (generally orange or red). These are

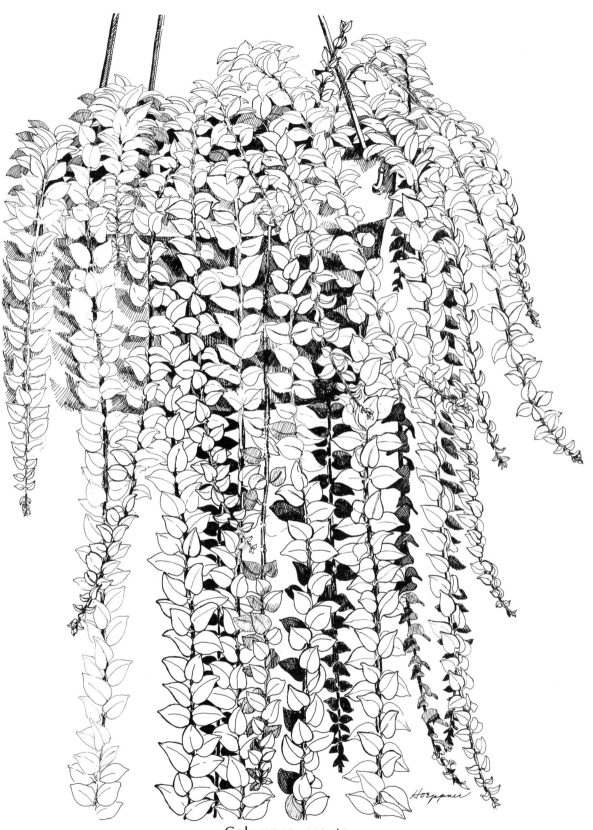

Columnea arguta

especially fine basket plants, and *C. arguta, C. gloriosa,* and *C. hirta* are outstanding. Grow them in a semi-sunny location, and keep them evenly moist.

Episcias, sometimes classed as foliage plants because of their exquisite multicolored leaves, also bear handsome starlike flowers in bright colors and are desirable additions to any indoor garden. There are hairy-leaved and smooth-leaved kinds in a rainbow of colors, and flowers are tubular and generally red, white, or yellow. The plants are graceful and bear strawberry-like stolons that cascade over the pot rim. They appreciate humidity and warmth and lots of water except in winter and fall when they can be grown somewhat dry.

Aeschynanthus, formerly known as Trichosporum, is a trailing plant with green leaves set opposite on stems that may reach 3 or 4 feet in length. At the tip end, clusters of scarlet flowers give the plant a festive look. The popular species are *A. lobbianum* or *A. pulchrum;* they need bright light and must dry out between waterings.

Achimenes are lovely bulbous plants, desirable but difficult. You must plant rhizomes (I have never seen young plants sold), and these are not easy to start into growth. Put six or eight into a 6-inch pot, and keep them warm (about 78°F.). When plants are 2- to 3-inches tall, pinch them back to encourage bushy growth. The tubular flowers are indeed pretty, and colors include white, rose, pink, purple and blue. Some varieties are dotted or veined with contrasting color.

In fall, allow plants to dry out, and store them in pots at 55°F. Replant in the spring in fresh soil, cover with ½ to 1 inch of soil and give them plenty of heat and moderate waterings. Achimenes are pretty basket plants but somewhat temperamental.

Kohlerias have lovely foliage and fine pink or red tubular flowers that add a bright note to any garden in the air. For all their beauty the plants are not difficult to grow. Keep them in bright light rather than sun and never allow them to become completely dry or they will die. Use room temperature water; cold water spots the foliage. The best ones to try in the hanging garden are *K. amabilis* and *K. bogotensis.*

With tiny leaves and pouch like reddish-orange flowers, *Hypocyrta strigillosa* has become very popular in the last year. It is an epiphytic plant that does not like too much sun or water. After blooming, let the plant rest a few months with soil barely moist.

Aeschynanthus pulchrum

It seems that most Gesneriads prefer indoor locations; they do not like wind or cold. However, in protected places on patios or terraces —Columnea, Aesychynanthus, Achimenes—can certainly be used. Move them indoors in early September or when temperatures go below 55°F. at night.

PHILODENDRONS

Philodendrons are perhaps the favorite indoor foliage plant in America. Yet for all their popularity, they are not ideal plants. Some of them are difficult to grow, and others, after a few years, become straggly and hardly appear attractive. Thus, careful selection of plants is vital in order to choose species that are easy to grow and always handsome. Philodendrons are native to Central and South America, and the family includes many climbers and trailers.

Some Philodendrons have large leaves, others have medium-sized leaves and still others, small leaves. For basket growing the small or medium-leaved plants are best. Lush verdent plants are preferred to the large-leaved species; the latter many times appear skeletal.

Even the basket Philodendrons (which are the easiest to grow) require special handling. They need bright light but little sunlight, and although they are tolerant of fluctuating temperatures they do require more than the ordinary amount of humidity, at least 30 per cent, to really thrive.

P. cordatum (oxycardium) is perhaps the best species. It has attractive heart-shaped leaves; and is a relatively fast-growing plant that fills a container in a few months. *P. hastatum*, one of the spear-shaped species, has thick, dark green, glossy leaves and with reasonable care will grow for years in a bright place. The varigated variety *P. hastatum variegatum* is somewhat more colorful with its green and yellow foliage. *P. mamei* and *P. sodiroi* are other species with lovely colored leaves that make good basket subjects. Avoid large-leaved species such as *P. pertusum* and *P. panduraeforme* and self-heading types such as *P. wendlandii* and *P. cannifolium*.

FERNS

Ferns in Victorian days were immensely popular and are just as popular now. They offer a wealth of green color for little money and care. However, because there are so many Ferns it is wise to select the ones that have some outstanding characteristics. Many have stiff dull green fronds and are to be avoided; several others are lush and emerald-green in color, with pendulous fronds that are superb. Ferns will grow in almost any situation for some time, but they do prefer bright light and a very rich humusy soil. Fronds are somewhat delicate, and if bruised will turn brown, and then the natural beauty of the plant is lessened. For this reason, most Ferns are better grown on a pedestal stand or in hanging baskets where the true beauty of the plant can be seen from all angles. A lopsided Fern is hardly handsome; it is the symmetrical rosette growth that is so appealing.

A very common Fern that tops my list for a hanging garden is the Rabbit's-foot Fern, *Davallia fejeensis*; it has creeping rootstock and attractive fronds. It is a dense plant and very appropriate for baskets. Keep the soil almost wet all year. Nephrolepis (the sword-fern) is another good candidate for basket growing. Almost all varieties of sword-fern are derived from *N. exaltata*, and these are countless varieties. My favorites include *N. exaltata* 'Veronica' and 'Fluffy Ruffles'. These are both lacy plants with a lovely, delicate appearance. *Adiantum cuneatum* is another good species and there are several varieties; most have dark green fronds and make stellar basket plants.

To me, Polypodiums are not as charming as the other Ferns; only one in the group, *P. aureum mandaianum* with its crested bluish fronds, is outstanding, Platycerium (staghorn-fern) is still another group; mature specimens are handsome, but they are difficult to grow and take many years to become established. Furthermore, they require heat and humidity, conditions which are generally lacking in most situations. For something different, try *Woodwardia orientalis* which has leathery fronds. An airy plant, it needs plenty of room. The holly Ferns (Cyrtomiums) with their dark green leaflets that resemble holly, are other good possibilities for baskets.

SUCCULENTS

These fine trailers are an overlooked group of plants that are ridiculously easy to grow. Because of their unusually colored leaves and intricate patterns, Succulents are excellent when something different is needed. Plants have a lovely texture, pretty blooms, and cover containers in a mound of color. For all their beauty, Succulents are amenable plants that are almost impossible to kill; they should be grown

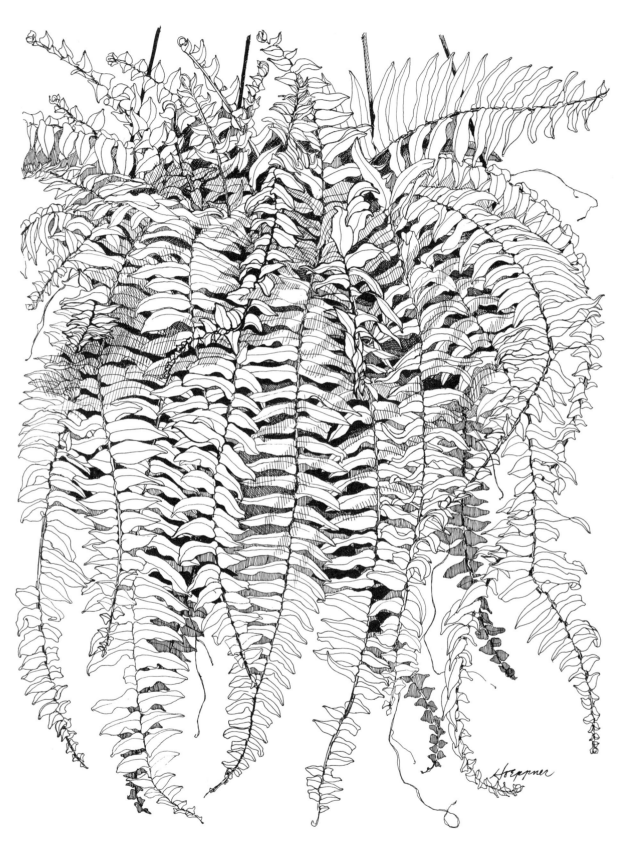

Nephrolepis exaltata

much more. Basically, all of them will respond well with only bright light. Allow them to dry out between waterings. Put several plants of the same kind into a basket for a lavish display. Baskets should be full, almost brimming, to be at their best. Hylocereus, Selenicereus, and Epiphyllums (orchid cactus) are large and by nature, pendant growers. They make impressive displays in baskets; the Christmas and Easter cacti are lovely, too. Some of the new varieties are spectacular in bloom; the plants almost covered with a cloud of flowers. To bloom these holiday plants keep soil moderately moist except in fall when roots should be somewhat dry and plants grown cool (50 to 55° F.) with 12 hours of uninterrupted darkness for a month to encourage bud formation.

The Mexican garden favorite *Sedum morganianum* (burro's tail) is a handsome oddity with gray-green, beadlike leaves. The "tails" can reach 6 to 7 feet. Easy to grow, this Sedum needs only bright light and an evenly moist soil, except in winter, when it can be grown somewhat dry. *S. sieboldii*, a common ground cover, takes on new airs when it is in a basket; it is a lovely pink halo of color in spring. *S. brevifolium* and *S. dasyphyllum* are other good trailers.

Aeoniums have lovely rosettes of green, copper, or red leaves and make splendid basket plants. They have been overlooked by gardeners, and yet they offer a lot of color for little effort. My favorites are: *A. caespitosum*, a low grower and *A. decorum*, which has tufted gray-green rosettes. Plants need some sun and a somewhat dry soil all year.

Crassulus are plants you often see in the houseplant section of florist shops, and within the group there are some fine trailers. These include: *C. deltoidea* (silver beads) with powdery gray leaves, *C. perforata* (necklace vine) with blue-gray foliage, and *C. schmidtii*, a delightful basket plant with green needle-like leaves.

Kalanchoe uniflora is another handsome Succulent and some of the Rhipsalis species with terete leaves and colorful berries are always desirable in baskets. *R. paradoxa* is my favorite.

Other lesser-known Succulents include *Kleinia pendula* with gray-green, almost blue stems, *Oscularia deltoides* with crips gray leaves and crowns of lavender flowers. Not to be left out is the wonderful oddity *Senecio rowleyanus*, a plant that looks like a mass of strings covered with green peas.

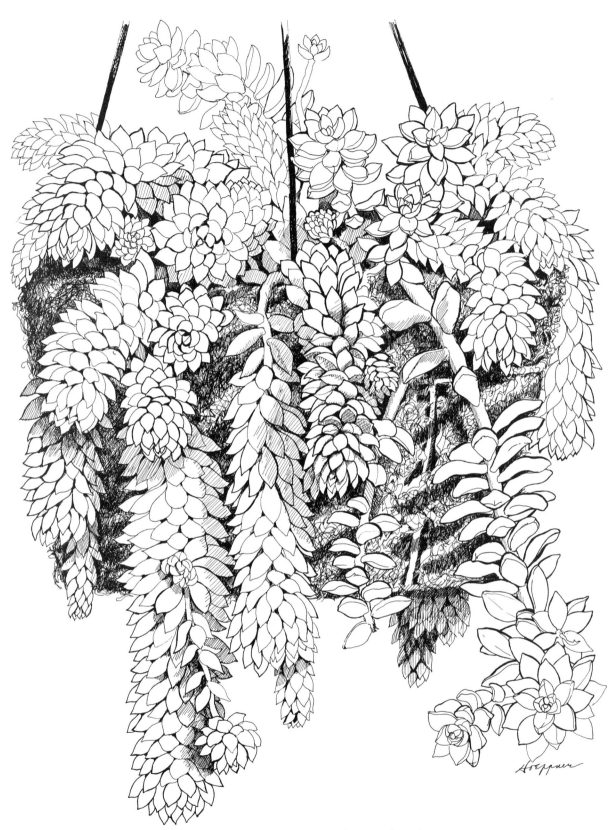

Sedum morganianum — Sedum adolphii

Sedum sieboldii

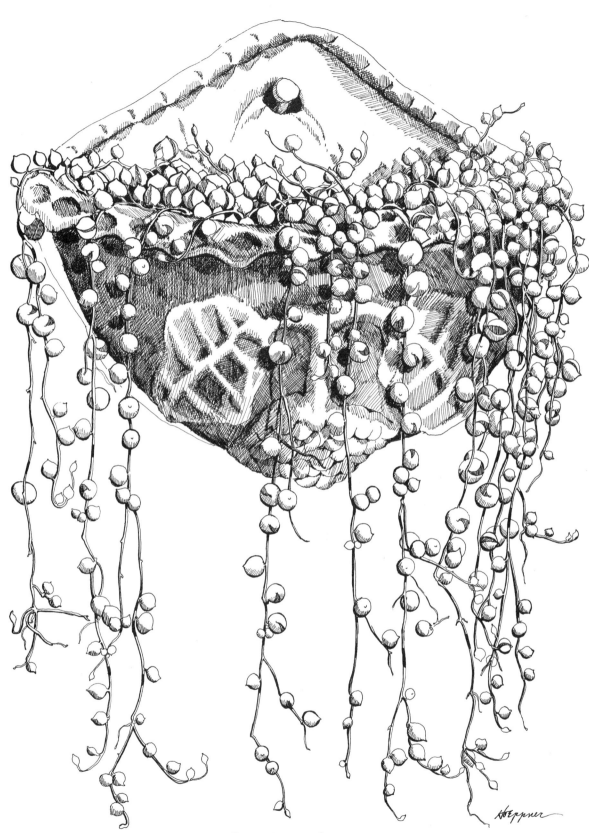

Senecio rowleyanus

Trailing succulents are wall decoration for an outdoor porch. In winter, plants are kept in a heated greenhouse. (Author photo)

Most plants mentioned here can be used indoors or out; minimum night temperature 55°F.

BROMELIADS

These are the plants often seen in public buildings and lobbies; they can tolerate adverse conditions. Of rosette or vase-shaped growth, Bromeliads are showy with bright flower bracts that are colorful for weeks. In the group are some excellent baskets plants because they put out numerous offshoots (small plants) and eventually make a lavish display.

These air plants from Brazil make the jump to your indoor garden with far less fuss than most plants. If you forget to water them for a few days they still survive because most of them have a bowl formation of leaves. Keep the vase filled with water and saturate the potting mix—osmunda—once a week. Put them in open-sides wire baskets or redwood boxes so the offshoots have space to grow.

To pot a Bromeliad, soak the osmunda overnight so that it is easy to work with. No drainage material is necessary in open-sided containers; set the plant in place and work the fiber into the center of the pot. Avoid setting the base of the plant too deep into the container

A specimen size Bromeliad (Bromelia balanse) hangs from a porch eave; plants are bright green with red centers. (Author photo)

and crushing the leaf cup. Some Bromeliads have spines on the leaf edges so wear gloves when working with them.

Bromeliads need large containers for some of them can grow quite tall. Furnish ample supports for them. Allow the plants to grow into specimens; this is when they are truly beautiful in baskets.

In summer grow them outdoors, the rest of the year keep them at a bright window in a cool place, about 55 to 60°F. at night.

Of the many fine Bromeliads, *Bromelia balanse* is outstanding. It has dark green toothed leaves to 36 inches, graceful and handsome. The center of the plant turns brilliant red at bloom time. Summer outdoors in bright light for a striking display on patio or terrace.

A plant similar in growth to Bromelia but with wider leaves is *Hohenbergia stellata*; the golden-green foliage is outstanding and if grown in sun the tall flower spike of lavender-blue blooms is stunning.

Two of the vase shaped Bromeliads are also suitable for baskets. *Streptocalyx poeppigii* with narrow spiny copper-red leaves and

Vriesia fenestralis, a regal plant with green leaves delicately figured with dark-green and purple lines. Put these in sun.

The popular *Neoregelia carolinae* can also be grown in the hanging garden. This rosette plant has dark green strap leaves with smooth edges. The center of the plant is fiery red at bloom time. It succeeds even in north light.

8. Orchids for Drama

Today Orchids are popular and can be grown successfully with a minimum of care, sometimes less care than needed for ordinary house plants. Orchids offer dramatic flowers, and they bloom at different times of the year—spring, summer, fall, winter—making them highly desirable plants. Many are summer blooming for outdoor color; others are fall and winter blooming for indoor color.

Many species are natural trailers with their cascading stalks of brightly colored flowers. *Dendrobium pierardii* is spectacular as a patio accent, and many dainty-flowered Gongoras make unique decoration. Large-flowered Stanhopeas and cascading Miltonias are other possibilities from this varied group of lovely plants.

Selection is vital with Orchids. Some need coolness, others warmth; some are deciduous, and several are evergreen. Many need very bright light to bloom, and others, such as *Coelogyne massangeana*, bear splendid beige flowers even in the shade.

Because many Orchids are arboreal in nature, the plants are more at home in baskets than in standard pots. In baskets suspended from ceilings they can naturaly enjoy bright light and circulation of air from all sides. Use slotted clay pots or redwood or wire baskets for orchids.

For potting plants in open containers, use a liner of sphagnum moss and then put in a layer of fir bark. Center the plant, and fill in and around it with bark; push the material into the pot working from the outside of the container to the center. Most species need firm potting. If you use slotted clay pots, put in a layer of shards

Dendrobium pierardi with large lavender flowers is a fountain of color in early spring. (Author photo)

over the drainage hole and then add bark and plants. *Do not immediately water newly potted plants.* Mist the pot and top of the bark for several days; in about a week roots will recover from the shock of transplanting and then plants can be watered.

For outdoors, choose the following spring and summer blooming species. Keep them well watered on sunny days. Do not water them in cloudy weather even if it is a prolonged spell. Minimum nighttime temperature for the following plants is 55°F. Some will tolerate a few nights of colder weather.

FOR SUN OR BRIGHT LIGHT

Dendrobium.

This is a large varied group of Orchids, with some evergreen and some deciduous. Flowers may be small or large, and they come in a wide range of colors, with perhaps yellow the predominant hue. The plants require bright light and much water. Allow them to dry out for a few weeks after they have flowered.

D. pierardii—Leaves 3 to 4 inches long, pale lilac flowers; semideciduous, spring.

D. moschatum—Six to 7 inch beige and maroon flowers; summer.

D. densiflorum—Small yellow flowers; summer.

D. superbum—Large lavender flowers on bare canes; rest after bloom. Spring.

D. wardianum—White and purple flowers; autumn.

Aerides.

Although these plants are upright growers with succulent leaves and aerial roots, the flowers are on long racemes. Color is generally magenta or pink, and most are sweetly scented (an added dividend). Grow in bright light (sunlight not necessary), and keep plants well watered all year.

A. affine—One inch white and deep-rose flowers; summer.

A. crassifolium—Dwarf purple flowers; summer.

A. odoratum—Creamy white flowers tipped with magenta; summer.

Gongora.

Curious small-to-medium orchids with broad plicated leaves and pendulous stems of inverted flowers, complex in structure. Color is generally beige to yellow. Rest plants after they bloom.

G. galeata—One-inch yellow flowers; summer.

G. quinquenervis—One-inch yellow and red flowers; spring.

Chysis.

Natural trailing orchids with broad green leaves and handsome waxy flowers in early spring. Keep fir bark evenly moist all year except for a few weeks after blooming when plants can be grown almost dry. Plants are easy to grow; mature specimens impressive.

C. laevis—A bounty of waxy beige-pink-and-white flowers.

Odontoglossum.

Orchids with long wands of flowers, hundreds to a stem, predominately yellow. Prefer coolness. Need sunlight and moist potting material all year.

O. grande—Seven-inch flowers, yellow and brown; fall.

O. harryanum—Five-inch flowers, yellow and brown; summer.

O. uroskinneri—Multicolored; spring and summer.

Dendrobium superbum

Chysis laevis

Oncidium.

Varied group of small-to-large plants with pendant stems and small flowers.

O. ornithorynchum—One-half to 1-inch lavender flowers; winter.

O. varicosum—yellow and red-brown flowers; autumn, winter and early summer.

ORCHIDS FOR SHADY LOCATIONS

Stanhopea.

Handsome evergreen plants with broad, dark green leaves and flower spikes that grow straight down. Blooms are mammoth (to 12 inches across) but only last a few days. Plants need sunlight and much water. Rest somewhat after bloom.

S. oculata—Seven-inch flowers; light yellow and oranges; late summer.

S. tigrina—Seven inch yellow-orange flowers, colors variable; summer.

S. wardii—Seven inch flowers; golden yellow blotched with red-purple.

Coelogyne.

A wonderful group of handsome plants with erect and mostly pendulous flower stems. Blooms are small to medium, mainly beige or tan in color. Keep watered all year.

C. cristata—Five inch flowers, pure white; winter.

C. dayana—Two-inch flowers, pale yellow; summer.

C. flaccida—One to 2 inch flowers, white and beige; needs rest; spring.

C. massangeana—One inch flowers, beige and brown; autumn and winter.

Cymbidiums (miniature)

Cousins to the large-flowered Cymbidiums so popular in California, these have handsome and erect grassy foliage and a bountiful crop of small colorful flowers on drooping stems. Need cool nights in

A hybrid evergreen cane type Dendrobium bears pendent stems with many blossoms; these are yellow with red centers. (Author photo)

late summer and early fall to bloom. Pot in cymbidium mix from suppliers. Hundreds of varieties available.

Militonia.

Upright growers with pendant sprays of pansy type flowers that are long-lasting. Plants grow all year so keep potting mix evenly moist at all times. Excellent patio decoration and easy to grow.

M. candida—Greenish-brown and yellow flowers in fall.

M. vexillaria—Exquisite rose-red flowers in summer.

Phalaenopsis.

Popular orchids with straplike foliage and graceful wands of flowers, open-faced and lovely. Called Moth-orchids, these like plenty of

On a pedestal stand, an Oncidium hybrid offers dramatic beauty with numerous pendent scapes and yellow flowers. (American Orchid Society photo)

shade and a moist atmosphere. Reduce watering somewhat after plants bloom.

P. amabilis—Large white flowers, many to a scape. Several varieties.

Trichopilia.

From Mexico and Brazil, these epiphytes have short upright green leaves and pendant flowers. There are about 25 species but only a few are outstanding.

T. suavis—Large creamy white flowers with red spots; spring blooming.

T. tortilis—Large flowers, more colorful than above species; highly desirable plant.

An easy to grow Orchid,
Trichopilia suavis is
splendid as a trailing plant;
it blooms in summer.
(Author photo)

For shady areas, a pendent
flowering Coelogyne orchid
furnishes brown-and-beige
color accent. (Author photo)

9. Basket Begonias ✒

Begonias make ideal basket plants, and there are hundreds of them. The choice runs from airy Angel-wings, with cascading clusters of flowers, to lush Rhizomatous types, with thick stemlike roots that skirt the surface of the pot. If you like velvety and whiskered foliage choose handsome Hirsute Begonias, and not to be forgotten are the everblooming Semperflorens that are a halo of color in a basket and the magnificent Tuberous Begonias, long-standing favorites.

TUBEROUS BEGONIAS

Tuberous Begonias are showoffs. With flamboyant flowers in bright colors, they are dramatic patio and porch decoration. The cascading flowers are breathtaking, and the plants give much satisfaction for little effort. Most important, they will reach perfection in bright light under porch roofs or eaves, places where other plants cannot grow. However, they will not bloom in total shade.

The summer-flowering Tuberous Begonias are called *B. tuberhybrida* and are intercrossed hybrids that produce large flowers on vigorous plants. There are several types available, but for hanging baskets the Multifloras are colorful, and the Pendula varieties with a natural trailing habit are best.

Although the plants have been extensively hybridized, the original breeding stock were species from the high elevation of the Andes mountains where coolness prevails. Today's plants still thrive with cool nights, plenty of good air circulation, and warm days.

Begonia tubers are at suppliers and nurseries in early March. To start them, put a 2-inch layer of equal parts of peat moss and sand

Trailing tuberous begonias are welcome additions to the summer scene. This one in a wire basket has hundreds of yellow flowers. (Vetterle & Reinelt photo)

in a shallow azalea pot or in a wooden flat. Set the tubers in place 2 inches apart and ½ inch deep with the dented side up. Cover them with about ¼ inch of the mix. Be sure the tuber is completely covered because roots develop from the bottom, sides, and tops. Place the tubers in bright light (no sunlight) in 60 to 70°F., and keep the rooting medium moist to the touch. Too much water will cause the tubers to rot, and too little water will produce weak growth. When the sprouts are almost 2 inches high (in about 2 to 3 weeks), shift them into shallow pots, two to three tubers in a container. Use a loose soil mixture of 2 parts loam to 1 part leaf mold, and move plants to a cooler place. Keep soil evenly moist.

About May plants are ready for hanging baskets. Put them in 8- or 10-inch containers; wire or redwood slatted baskets are satisfactory. Line the baskets with sphagnum moss, and fill with 2 parts garden loam, 1 part leaf mold, and a handful of sand. Suspend the baskets from roof or porch eaves or from wall brackets unless there is some scattered sunlight.

Tuberous Begonias will survive the heat of the day, but they must have cool nights (55 to 60°F.). If summer days are very hot, mist the area around the plants but not the leaves. Water plants heavily on bright days but not as much in cloudy weather. When they are growing well, start using a fertilizer (10-10-5) mixed half strength every second week.

Once growing, and before flower buds appear, pinch out plants to encourage branching and lush growth. To look their best, containers should be full; remove faded flowers and leaves quickly.

After flowering, when leaves turn yellow and dry, water Begonias sparingly, and let growth continue for as long as possible. Then take plants inside and lift the tubers from the pot. Dust them with powdered charcoal and store them in open trays or boxes where air can circulate around them. Keep cool (45 to 50°F.), dark, and dry until repotting time in the spring. Tubers can then be divided to start them again.

If you do not have the time to start tubers, seedlings are available in April at nurseries. These are ready for basket containers, so only one planting is necessary.

Begonia 'Cleopatra' makes a fine basket subject and is easy to grow. (Joyce R. Wilson photo)

In a redwood basket, Begonia foliosa makes a charming picture. (Roche photo)

The Multiflora Begonias are smaller and more compact than the giant-flowering Tuberhybrida types. They bloom profusely (with masses of brilliant color) and will tolerate some sunlight. The flowers are single or semidouble, and excessive pinching of young growths is not necessary. Leaves are bronze or gren, slender and pointed, and a perfect foil for the colorful blooms. Some of the Multifloras have been bred with the larger camellia-type Tuberhybridas, and other hybrids appear from time to time. Even though there are named varieties available, most Begonias are sold by color rather than specific name.

The Pendula Begonias are variously called trailing or hanging types or sometimes 'Lloydi' Begonias. There are also picotee types that have small delightful blooms edged with color. The modern hybrids are impressive plants, and baskets are almost smothered in flowers. They

An Angel-wing Begonia with ornamental foliage is part of this patio. The variety is B. 'Ellen Dee.' (Mrs. Carl Meyer photo)

need a more protected place than the Multifloras and are sensitive to too much sun and wind. Flowers come in an array of lovely colors and plants are generally ordered by color rather than by name.

Other Begonias

This list includes some Angel-wing and Rhizomatous species. You will find them easier to grow than tuberous types and they are evergreen all year. Keep soil evenly moist and plants enjoy a bright place.

'Alpha Gere'—Wedge-shaped leaves and small white flowers.
'Limminghei'—Pointed, shiny green leaves and red flowers. Needs warmth and bright light.

'Marjorie Daw'—Wavy green foliage and pink flowers. Keep out of
    sun.

'd'Artagnan'—One of the best hairy-leaved Begonias. Forest-green
    foliage. Dense grower; keep somewhat dry in bright light.

'Elsie M. Frey'—Metallic-green, red-lined leaves.

'Ivy Ever'—Heart-shaped, dark green glossy leaves, pink flowers.
    Keep somewhat dry in bright light. No sunlight.

'Shippy's Garland'—Crinkled leaves and pink flowers.

'Lulandi'—Lovely angel-wing with small leaves and pink blooms.

'Orange Dainty'—Dark green leaves, handsome blooms.

'Maphil' (Cleopatra)—Exquisite variegated foliage and dainty pink
    blooms.

'Helen W. King'—Bronze-green leaves and pink flowers.

As mentioned, wax Begonias, sometimes called everblooming, are
indeed lovely in baskets, and so are some of the exquisite Rex Begonias with their almost iridescent foliage.

10. Trailing Geraniums ✍

The ivy-leaved Geraniums *Pelargonium peltatum* and its varieties
are graceful basket plants. Not as lush as Fuchsias or as vibrant in
color as Begonias, the Ivy Geraniums nevertheless have an airy
charm. The plants offer a bounty of color for the basket gardener—
pink, rose, lavender, purple, cerise, and white-tinted kinds. Suspended from window gardens indoors, or outdoors from roof eaves
and overhangs, they provide handsome decoration.

Except in regions of extreme heat and humidity, these Geraniums
will be a rainbow of color from May until about October. Plants need
some sun during the day; in the shade, bloom will be sparse.

Care of Plants

Soil is perhaps the key to growing Geraniums successfully; drainage must also be perfect and plants will suffer if soil becomes sour.
Use a friable neutral mix of 1 part garden loam, 1 part peat moss, and

Ivy geraniums are superlative in baskets or hanging pots. (Author photo)

a handful of pebbles or perlite per pot. Large containers (at least 10 inches in diameter and 4 to 5 inches deep) are best for Geraniums. Line the container with sphagnum moss, and put in a layer of soil and some crushed stone or perlite. Put plants in place at a slight angle near the edge of the basket; use three or four plants. Fill in and around with soil, press it into place until it is firm and leave an inch of space at the top of the container so that watering will be easy.

Geraniums need somewhat less moisture than most basket plants. Too much or too little water causes leaves to drop or disease. Allow plants to dry out between waterings, but when you do water Geraniums, do it thoroughly until excess water drains freely from the bottom of the pot.

Once the plant is growing, trim and cut rangy and straggly growth. Shape and prune the Geranium so that it is neat and attractive; new leaves will appear in a short time below the cuts. Stop cutting and pinch back the plant about 3 months before you want it to bloom.

Do not give Geraniums too much fertilizer; if the soil has adequate nutrients to start with, feeding is almost unnecessary. Plants fed heavily seem more prone to insect attack than those that are not fed. However, light fertilizing is fine; perhaps once a month during the growing season fertilize with a weak solution of 10-10-5.

Geraniums are perennials and in most areas must be stored in winter. An unheated but not freezing garage was where I put my plants when I lived in Illinois. In October, when the outdoor season is over, I remove the plants from their containers, but I try to keep the rootball intact. I dry out plants before storing them on a shady dry shelf.

Here a robust ivy geranium completely hides the container with a shower of pink blooms. (Calif. Assoc. of Nurserymen photo)

Geraniums in assorted containers decorate a patio-entry area. (Joyce R. Wilson photo)

I allow the plants to die back naturally before storing them, but I do not cut them back. At monthly intervals I moisten the rootballs somewhat. When it is time to set the Geraniums in baskets again, I cut them back and repot them in fresh soil. There are many variations on storing the plants. Some gardeners put the rootballs in plastic bags; others remove all soil at the end of the growing season and store them in bags. No matter how you winter your Geraniums, be sure that they have some moisture during the rest period.

Although it is unlikely that a few baskets of Geraniums will be attacked by pests and insects, some general hints are included here—just in case. Perhaps the most common condition to attack plants is edema. This appears as a disease but is really a cultural problem. The symptoms are water-soaked spots that appear on leaves that eventully turn yellow and fall. To avoid this condition, do not overwater the plants in dull cloudy weather. Be sure they have plenty of light and air, and as mentioned, allow soil to dry out thoroughly between waterings.

Spider mites may occasionally attack trailing Geraniums, and these tiny insects leave a grayish-yellow streaked appearance on leaves.

Hot, dry conditions encourage spider mites, so try to keep humidity high in hot weather. If this doesn't work, hose down plants every day (in the morning) for a few weeks. If the problem still is not solved, apply a light application of Malathion insecticide.

Bacterial leaf spot, stem rot, and botyritis blight seldom attack Geraniums in the home. Once again, good culture is the best preventative, with plenty of air and light. If, however, plants yellow and wilt rapidly or gray-brown masses cover blossoms or leaves, discard plants and start again.

BEST GERANIUMS FOR HANGING BASKETS
'Apricot Queen'—Double soft salmon-pink to white flowers.
'Barbara Wirth'—Striking double cerise blooms.
'Carlos Uhden'—Double bright red flowers with white center.
'Charles Turner'—A good double large rose-pink variety. Robust grower.
'Comtesse de Grey'—Semidouble soft pink-violet-marked flowers.
'Double Lilac White'—One of the best whites.
'Giant Salmon'—Very large flowers; compact reliable plant.
'La France'—Double large purple-marked lavendar flowers. One of the best.
'Mexican Beauty'—Semidouble dark red blooms; spectacular.
'Mrs. Banks'—Semidouble white flowers with lilac undertones.
'Sybil Holmes'—Double rose-pink flowers; compact, almost dwarf.

11. Fuchsias ✐

Fuchsias, sometimes called lady's eardrops, are well known as basket plants although there are some upright and shrub types in the family. Yet it is the lovely cascading varieties with blazing colorful flowers that capture the summer spotlight. With their long season of bloom, Fuchsias are undemanding and make a handsome display in shaded areas where other plants fail. A well-grown Fuchsia is a cloud of living color wit hundreds of flowers obscuring the container.

Fuchsias always make good basket subjects; they have lush growth and a bounty of flowers. (Joyce R. Wilson photo)

We mainly think of Fuchsias as purple or purple-red although there are now many fine varieties with all white or pink blossoms. These are not as floriferous as other varieties and somewhat more difficult to grow, but they have immense charm.

The majority of Fuchsias are from Central and South America, which has high altitudes and cool nighttime temperatures. Even during the summer, cool evenings make Fuchsias thrive. Some new varieties will tolerate somewhat warmer nights.

Whether used as patio accents or as pot plants, to be grown successfully the plants need plenty of water, a partially shady place, and weak feeding. Most Fuchsias thrive in shade, but there are some varieties—the small single-flowering types—that tolerate late afternoon sunlight. However, all need a protected place because winds and drafts can harm plants.

The trailing Fuchsias need training and pinching or else they grow rampant. They are basically fast growing and fill a container with lush foliage within a few months. To grow plants, start with cuttings; take three or four of one variety (such as 'Swingtime' or 'Cascade') for each container (or buy young plants already started at nurseries). With weaker-growing varieties such as 'Enchanted' and 'Pastel', you may need five or six cuttings for a basket.

Prepare baskets with care. If containers have openings in them—redwood baskets or wire ones—line them with 1 inch of sphagnum moss. For standard clay pots, use a liner of peat moss. Then place a layer of soil on the bottom of the container, and put the plants in place at a 45-degree angle around the edge of the pot. (Try not to disturb the rootballs.) Work soil in between the rootballs; pack it in tightly so that no air pockets form within the soil. Fill the container to about 1 inch from the top so that there is space for ample water.

CARE OF PLANTS

Good soil is an absolute must for Fuchsias. They are rapid growers and soon deplete the soil of nutrients. Start with a soil mix of 1/3 leaf mold, 1/3 topsoil, and 1/3 cow manure. Add some bone meal to encourage flower production and some peat moss to increase soil acidity and to hold moisture.

The best time to start plants is in the spring, after the danger of frost is over. It may take a few weeks for new Fuchsias to adjust to your growing conditions. They may lose leaves, and stems may appear limp. Have patience, and do not try to force them into growth with feeding; eventually, they will regain their vigor.

Plants outdoors in natural air currents dry out quickly, so water Fuchsias copiously, especially on hot days. Soil should be always evenly moist. If you are not at home to tend your Fuchsias daily, line the inside of the basket with plastic. This will help to hold moisture in the soil. Be sure to punch some holes in the plastic so that excess water can drain. Then insert the sphagnum moss over the plastic.

The hybrid varieties such as 'Cascade' and 'Swingtime' are so vigorous and floriferous that if they are allowed to grow naturally their branches and flowers sometimes become tangled and the plant looks unkempt. With such varieties small collars (used for African violets) or pieces of cane can be plunged into the soil to protrude over the edge and support stems.

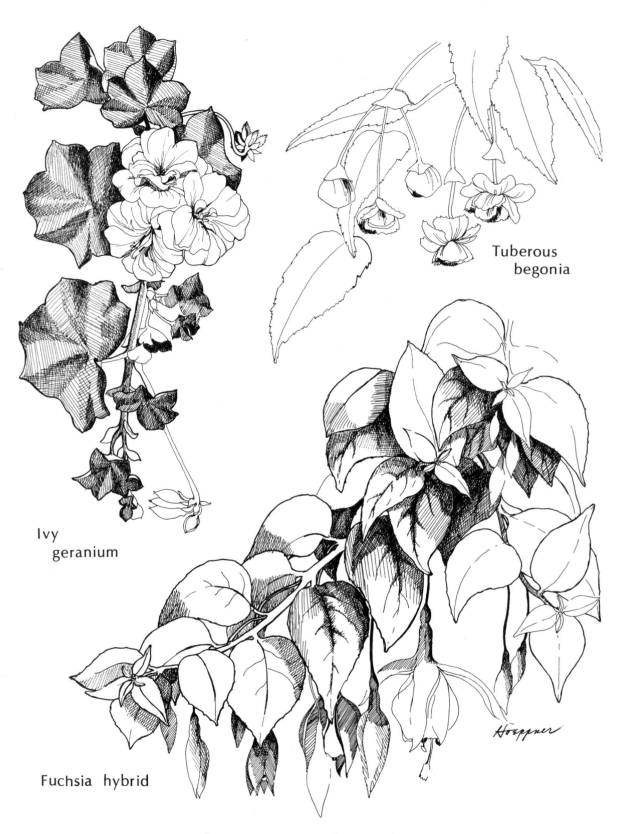

Tuberous
begonia

Ivy
geranium

Fuchsia hybrid

The Best Basket Plants

In a redwood basket, this fine fuchsia provides summer color in a patio. (Author photo)

Fuchsias are greedy plants and demand feeding. However, some rules should be kept in mind when using fertilizers. Never feed a dry plant, a sick plant, or a recently potted plant. Wait about 2 weeks until it is established. Once a week leach out soil with water so that fertilizers do not become locked into the soil and burn the roots. My feeding schedule for Fuchsias is every other watering in June, July, and August, using a 10-10-5 commercial fertilizer, well diluted.

Fuchsias are rarely attacked by insects, but they do suffer from leaf drop. This is a cultural problem caused either by too much fertilizer or not enough water. At no time during its growth should a Fuchsia be without water. If dry for a time and then watered, the moisture taken by the roots causes pressure on the cells of the leaves and they drop.

Most gardeners have a lovely display of hanging Fuchsias for summer and then dispose of them. This is not economical or necessary because Fuchsias are easy to carry over the winter. There is no reason why the same plant cannot be a lovely display the next summer.

From about September on gradually decrease water and let the plants start to rest. Keep the soil barely moist. Let the leaves fall and

Baskets of fuchsias decorate this entrance area. (Roche photo)

the remaining buds and flowers drop. When the plant is almost bare, put it in a frost-free place—a garage or basement—but don't forget it. About twice a month give it a thorough watering. If you find the plant starting new growth, move it to a cooler (but not freezing) place.

In spring, don't be too anxious to get the Fuchsia growing. Wait until the end of May (this varies with individual regions), and then start the plant again. Put it in a shady airy spot, and as soon as you see new growth, repot the plant in fresh soil. In a few weeks, when growth is underway, prune the Fuchsia; cut it back to 3 or 4 inches. Now it is ready for its season of growth and another summer of color.

BEST FUCHSIAS FOR HANGING BASKETS

'Ben Hur'—Purple, pink, and white double flowers. A good one.

'Berkeley'—Large double flowers, pale rose and rose-red. Prolific bloomer.

'Bon Bon'—Double pale pink and white flowers.

'Butterfly'—Single flowers, crimson and rose. Striking.

'Cascade'—Single white and carmine medium-sized flowers. Vigorous.

'Creole'—Double crimson and maroon flowers. Dramatic.

'Kimberley'—Deep blue and pink semidouble flowers.

'Lullaby'—Double pink and lavendar flowers. Easy to grow.

'La Fiesta'—Striking white and purple blooms.

'Mandarin'—Orange and carmine blooms.

'Marinka'—A favorite, with red and maroon flowers.

'Parisienne'—Blue-violet and pink flowers. Prolific bloomer.

'Red Jacket'—Large and profuse flowers.

'San Pablo'—Rose-pink and lavendar blooms.

'Shady Lane'—Large lilac-blue and rose flowers. A choice one.

'Sweet Sixteen'—Rose and pink blooms. Vigorous grower.

'Trailing King'—Single small flowers, magenta and rose.

Many new varieties appear periodically; check local nurseries and suppliers' catalogues.

Appendix

CONTAINERS

Containers for hanging plants are at most nurseries and garden centers and include the standard terra cotta pot in many designs and sizes; ceramic pottery, and decorative tubs and dishes of various designs. You will also find drip-saucers for pots and hanging devices —chain, rope, or wire—at garden shops.

Your local hardware store will have screws or eyehooks or other necessary hardware for hanging the containers.

PLANT SOCIETIES

African Violet Society of America
P.O. Box 1326
Knoxville, Tenn. 37901

American Begonia Society
1510 Kimberly Ave.
Anaheim, Calif. 92802

American Orchid Society
Botanical Museum of Harvard University
Cambridge, Mass. 02138

The Bromeliad Society
1811 Edgecliff Drive
Los Angeles, Calif.

Saintpaulia International
P.O. Box 10604
Knoxville, Tenn. 37919

Write for membership information and fees.

WHERE TO BUY PLANTS

Most trailing plants are available at florists or nurseries in the house plant section. Specialty plants such as Orchids, Bromeliads, Geraniums, Succulants and others can be ordered by mail from the following suppliers:

Alberts & Merkel Bros. Inc. P.O. Box 537 Boynton Beach, Fla. 33435	*Orchids, bromeliads.*
Burgess Seed & Plant Co. 67 E. Battle Creek St. Galesburg, Mich. 49053	*All kinds of house plants.*
W. Atlee Burpee Co. Philadelphia, Pa. 19132	*All kinds of house plants.*
Fischer Greenhouses Linwood, N.J. 08221	*Gesneriads.*
Hausermans Orchids Box 363 Elmhurst, Ill. 60218	*Orchids.*
Henriettas Nursery 1345 N. Brawley Fresno, Calif. 93705	*Cactus and Succulents.*
Margaret Ilgenfritz Box 665 Monroe, Mich. 48161	*Orchids.*
Johnson Cactus Gardens 2735 Olive Hill Rd. Fallbrook, Calif. 92028	*Cactus and succulents.*

Logees Greenhouses
5 North St.
Danielson, Conn. 06239

House plants.

Merry Gardens
Camden, Me. 04843

House plants.

George W. Park Seed Co. Inc.
Box 31
Greenwood, S.C. 29646

House plants.

Wilson Bros.
Roachdale, Ind. 46172

Geraniums.

BOOKS TO READ

The Joy of Geraniums, Helen Van Pelt Wilson, Barrows.

Fuchsias, Stanley J. Wilson, St. Martins Press.

Rare Orchids Everyone Can Grow, J. Kramer, Doubleday

Bromeliads, the Colorful House Plants, J. Kramer, Van Nostrand

Wonderful World of Bulbs, Bebe Miles, Van Nostrand

Gesneriads and How to Grow Them, Edited by Peggie Schultz,
     Diversity Books

Cacti and Succulents, Indoors & Out, Martha Van Ness, Van Nostrand

Begonias, Indoors & Out, J. Kramer, E. P. Dutton

Foliage Plants for Indoor Gardens, James Underwood Crockett,
     Doubleday